TOWARDS A SCIENCE OF PEACE

TOWARDS A SCIENCE OF PEACE

Turning Point in Human Destiny

by

Theo*dore* F. *Ferdinand* Lentz, PH.D.

Lecturer in Education and International Understanding
Formerly Associate Professor of Education
Washington University, St. Louis, U.S.A.

With a Foreword by
Dr. Julian Huxley

BOOKMAN ASSOCIATES INC.,
NEW YORK 3

FIRST PUBLISHED IN 1955 BY
HALCYON PRESS (BARNET) LTD.
15 NEW ROW, ST. MARTIN'S LANE, LONDON, W.C.2

Second Printing in the
United States of America
1961

Printed in the U.S.A.
Noble Offset Printers, Inc.
New York 3, N.Y.

FOREWORD

It gives me great pleasure to write a brief foreword to Professor Lentz's book *Towards A Science Of Peace*. Professor Lentz has done a most useful work in pointing out the intimate relationship between science and peace, in the full sense of scientific method, knowledge, attitude, and application on the one hand, and on the other the peaceable realization of human possibilities through peaceful co-operation, as well as the mere prevention of war.

I was especially impressed by the points he makes about the existing obstacles to the use of science for constructive or positive peace—the backward-looking view which overrates tradition and existing knowledge (though it must be emphasized that a vast betterment could be achieved merely by the full application of existing knowledge); the failure to grasp the immense possibilities of future discovery; and the popular misconceptions of science as being primarily concerned with physics and chemistry or as being merely a provider of gadgets and machines and 'wonder drugs', or as leading mainly to greater destructiveness in war.

His emphasis on the human sciences (social sciences, psychology, anthropology, etc.) and the need of exploring their possibilities with a view to discovering better methods of social and economic co-operation and greater human fulfilment is basic, and his passages on this subject should be read and pondered by all who look forward to the establishment of One World on a constructive and peaceful basis.

There is one point on which I would perhaps go further than Professor Lentz. In his practical suggestions he concentrates mainly on the idea of the direct investigation and mobilization of opinion for peace on the basis of science. I feel that the indirect effect of science, in creating a new dynamic of ideas, may be equally and possibly more important.

Perhaps I may be permitted to amplify this point. We are all aware of the fact that some sort of ideology, whether religious or socio-political, is an indispensable organ of every organized human society; and further that our ideologies in large measure determine the direction of our thoughts and actions, dictate our individual and social goals, and provide much of the driving force of our lives. Further, most thinking men and women are beginning to feel that today a new ideology is needed, a new orientation of thought and action, which on the one hand shall be in harmony with scientific knowledge and method, and on the other hand shall be adapted to the new conditions and necessities of the modern world, notably the prevention of war and mass destruction, the development of a co-operative supranational or transnational system and effort of world development, the control of population growth, and the conservation and proper utilization of world resources.

Professor Lentz rightly stresses the need for wider dissemination of knowledge and for fuller discussion of scientific facts and ideas at all levels of society—in other words for a wider use of the basic scientific principle of free discussion in the confident belief that it will lead to fuller truth and right action.

I feel that this world effort of discussion and comprehension and dissemination should concern itself largely with the facts of science, human as well as natural, in so far as they are relevant to the central problem of human destiny and with the grasping of their practical and ideological implications and consequences.

After all, the present is the first period in the history of the world in which man has been able to attain a reasonably accurate, comprehensive, and scientifically-based picture of his destiny; for this is the first period in which science has been extended to give us adequate knowledge of nature, including the stellar universe, the earth, the behaviour of matter, and the evolution of life; of man, including the peculiarities and possibilities of human nature, man's achievements and limitations, and his cultural and social history; and of the relation between these two, which defines man's place in nature and gives a picture of his possible role in the universe. This has never previously been possible, because science had not yet extended its field to cover the psychological (intellectual, aesthetic, and spiritual) and social aspects of reality as manifested in man.

At last, however, we have a scientifically-based picture of human destiny, in the place of the mythological and theological inventions and philosophical speculations of earlier ages. That destiny, it now appears, is to be the agent or instrument of the evolutionary process on this planet, the sole organism capable of realizing any major evolutionary advance in the earth's long future.

When we study the problem more in detail, taking into account the limitations as well as the possibilities of nature and man, we are at once forced to certain ideological and practical conclusions —for instance, that the overriding aim of mankind as a species must be the fulfilment of more possibilities by a greater number of highly developed individuals; that this aim can be more efficiently pursued in so far as we enlarge the single world pool of knowledge and the unitary frame work of ideas initiated by the march of modern science, and make it available to and operative in an increasing number of human beings. Further, that a greater range of possibilities can be realized through a wide variety of cultural opportunities and achievements, both within and between nations; so that a pattern of variety-in-unity is to be aimed at— cultural diversity within a unified intellectual frame work. Furthermore, that the task will be most efficiently carried out, not by competition or one-sided exploitation, but as a co-operative partnership in the single business of world development.

Such a picture of human destiny has many other implications and dictates many other conclusions—as regards population policy, for instance; and the role of the arts in national and international life; and the need for a generous extension of research in the human sciences and studies; and so on. But these are precisely the points which a worldwide effort of thought and discussion, such as Professor Lentz and I both envisage as a present necessity, will inevitably bring out and clarify.

There are still a number of natural scientists who are opposed to the extension of science to human affairs, often because they fear that it will then lose the accuracy and razor-edged certitude that it has achieved in the physical world. And there are many humanists and idealists who are equally opposed to such an extension, often because they are afraid of human values being denatured, so to speak, by what they regard as the cold and impersonal methods of science. Such fears are, I am sure, groundless: in the long run nothing but good can come from the marriage of scientific method with human values and ideals. To any such doubter, to the increasing number of people who are no longer satisfied with the world's traditional ideologies, and to all those who are profoundly perturbed by the threat of suicidal war, I commend Professor Lentz's book.

JULIAN HUXLEY

April 1954

PREFACE

PEACE has become a dangerous word. To evade that for which the word should stand, however, is far more dangerous. This book is based upon the twofold assumption that, practically speaking, the road to peace is not now known, but that it can be discovered if enough of us make it our main business to look for it. No blueprint is presented here for peace action, but rather a proposal for peace research action. This is a radical proposal for a new and profound approach to an exceedingly important and baffling problem.

We have tried to write this book from an overall human point of view, i.e., with global perspective. We have tried to escape the restrictions of a provincial background and a national point of view. We are sure our efforts here have been only partially successful. For this we apologize. Many of the concrete illustrations, as well as the idioms of language, can be constant reminders to the reader that world citizenship, in the psychological and spiritual sense, as well as legal, is still largely an ideal only. Against this we all must continue to struggle.

This is not, strictly speaking, a scientific book, but a book about science. It is a treatise on thought and action prerequisite to science for peace. Documentation has been largely omitted, partly out of necessity and partly in the interest of succinctness in the total ideological and theoretical presentation. For report on research thus far carried on in the field of human relations, the reader is referred to other books, such as, *Tensions Affecting International Understanding* by Otto Klineberg, *Human Relations In a Changing World* by Alexander Leighton, and *The Proper Study of Mankind* by Stuart Chase.

The writing of this book has been the major activity of the Attitude Research Laboratory over the past six years. The Laboratory is sponsored by the Character Research Association of St. Louis. Any royalties which may result from publication of this book are hereby assigned to the treasury of this non-profit organisation, incorporated under the laws of the State of Missouri, U.S.A.

The precise authorship of this book is difficult to describe. Over a period of six years, it is impossible to account for all the persons who enthusiastically participated in this enterprise. The greater credit goes to members of the Character Research Association, who furnished intellectual and moral support, as well as financial. For all this I am sincerely grateful. I am especially indebted to Joan Lyon Paul who, as secretarial associate, gave full time to this and related tasks for a period of more than four years.

I acknowledge also my debt to a great many of my students and others who participated in an uncounted number of Socratic dialogues on peace and related subjects. Much of the preliminary thinking for this treatise developed over some two decades of teaching and conferring while I was a member of the faculty of Washington University of St. Louis. In 1948, I was granted a sabbatical leave of one year for purposes of working on this book. This leave was continued through four subsequent years on the basis of one-fourth time employment. For this provision I am grateful.

For kind permission to quote, thanks and acknowledgments are due the authors and publishers of the following books: *No Place to Hide*, by David Bradley (Little, Brown & Co.); *The Proper Study of Mankind*, by Stuart Chase (Harper & Bros.); *Problems of Men*, by John Dewey (Philosophical Library); *Sweden: Champion of Peace*, by David Hinshaw (G. P. Putnam's Sons); *Human Relations in a Changing World*, by Alexander Leighton (E. P. Dutton & Co.); *Social Research*, by George Lundberg (Longmans, Green & Co.); *Human Nature and Enduring Peace*, by Gardner Murphy (Society for the Psychological Study of Social Issues & Houghton Mifflin).

THEO. F. LENTZ

ATTITUDE RESEARCH LABORATORY
  ST. LOUIS
July 1954

PREFACE
to Second Printing

The tides of time are still outrunning our hopes for peace. Although the political and scientific scene has changed since 1954 the situation is still critical if not desperate. The fashions of thought and the prevailing attitudes of most men, both lay and scientific, have not yet caught up with the basic thesis of this book that the all-powerful method of science must be invoked to cope with man's unprecedented political and military danger. As one reflects over the challenge of our subtitle it is clearly apparent that the turning point in human destiny has not yet been reached. However, we did not prophesy. We cannot now prophesy. We did recommend. We recommend still that humanity's greatest ungrasped opportunity is that of peace research.

In the intervening seven years the physical scientific technology has continued to accelerate. The complications, not to say confusions, in international relations have not abated. Our thesis continues ever more valid in the light of the world's big events. Those which are threats to our human security are major. Those which give us hope and assurance are still minor. As of this writing the United Nations, though much more entrenched in men's thoughts and more established in the value patterns of many, could still be made totally ineffectual through a mad impulse of one or another of the giant parties to the Cold War. And even though it survive and continue at its present level of strength there is little support for the hope that it could override sudden and surprise surges toward World War III. Mankind continues politically to muddle through with one foot in jet-rocket propulsion transportation and the other foot in the diplomatic oxcart.

As over against this dour picture from the military and political point of view the reader can find listed in the postscript at the end of this volume a number of small but significant recent developments looking towards a science of peace. In the causation of several of these our book has played a significant role. Two significant financial contributions resulted directly or indirectly from the reading of these pages to say nothing of a great many smaller beginnings whose potential outcomes are yet to be determined. Thus, it is most satisfying to have these verifications of our initial hypothesis that there exists a vast potential will for peace and peace research—a potential will to supply the essentials of a science of peace—essentials moral, intellectual, and financial.

One of the author's greatest personal rewards has been the joy of meeting like-minded enthusiasts whose identification has resulted from the reading of this book. To these and many others yet to be identified this second printing is dedicated.

CONTENTS

1. THE SETTING—MANKIND AT THE CROSSROADS 1

    The human race seems sick and unsuited to choose between sanity and suicide. Through inadvertence and ignorance, men are making unprecedented preparation for unprecedented physical and social calamity. This book proposes that we emphasize and extend science as a method for finding the remedy.

2. A CRISIS IN CULTURE 8

    Man is the victim of a vast dynamic culture which lacks unity and balance. This culture consists of an enormous complex of conflicting values, unwieldy organizations, extensive but one-sided knowledge and technology, and a vast array of powerful tools for physical construction and destruction of miraculous and deadly proportions. Man can only save himself by redirecting his culture through new uses of his intelligence at higher levels of co-operation.

3. SOCIETY MISORGANIZED 19

    Man as an individual is helpless, and as a group is ill organized to achieve the greater destiny which his physical environment and his social and psychological nature make possible. A vast pattern of ill-directed and powerful institutions deprive him of his primitive freedom and co-ordinate his efforts for gigantic and disastrous antagonisms. Men seem ill prepared by attitude and information for the global solidarity required for survival and continuous progress in the atomic age.

4. SCIENCE IN MISORDER 36

    The tragic plight of mankind at the present moment is due to an ever-widening discrepancy in two lines of development; namely, physical power and social harmony, a fact which makes conflict ever more intolerably dangerous and disastrous. This discrepancy is due to the uneven application of the scientific method to the two areas of physical and human relations. 'Science has found out the right things in the wrong order'

(Raymond Fosdick). To remedy this, a profound redirection of human intellectual energies is required. This in turn requires some sharp revisions in our attitudes and ideas.

5. IDEOLOGICAL BLOCKADES TO A SCIENCE OF PEACE   56

Scientific attitude toward peace is blocked by two interlocking assumptions. One is that we already know all we need to know. The other is that scientific intelligence is not suited to develop the kind of wisdom that we now lack. This latter assumption is due to false assumptions regarding the nature of attitude and the nature of science. However, scientific method is potentially applicable to all systematically observable behaviour including human behaviour—attitudinal, emotional, or otherwise.

6. ARTICLES OF FAITH   85

For work towards a science of peace, one needs
 1. Faith in the possibility of striking progress in the democratic *harmonization* of human purposes.
 2. Faith in the utility of *facts* as yet undiscovered.
 3. Faith in their discoverability by the utmost use of human *intelligence*.
 4. Faith in the creative evolution and redirection of *scientific method* of research.
 5. Faith in the existence and applicability of the *motive* of universal human betterment to supplant the motive of partisan utility superimposed upon the motive of pure science.

7. WHAT IS MEANT BY A SCIENCE OF PEACE?   105

The method of science when fundamentally conceived is highly suited to the problem of peace when conceived in psychological and political and operational terms. Scientific research is a process in which disciplined curiosity makes utmost use of intelligence to formulate, develop, and progressively answer meaningful and relevant questions by the aid of purposeful observation and reason. Science of peace represents part of the much needed democratization of science.

8. OUTLINING THE RESEARCH   119

A tentative outline, of a broad scientific programme of international and opinion-attitude research, for identifying and exposing democratically and co-operatively the mutual misunderstandings and other factors which lead to international conflict and slaughter, is presented.

CONTENTS

> This illustrative programme demonstrates that social science planning of wide scope and specific relevance is feasible.

9. **Speed and Manpower** — 150

> Is there time? Are men available? The factors which affect the speed of particular sciences can be discerned. One of these—the number of men on the job—is susceptible to deliberate and direct control. The human resource, some trained but mostly untrained, for an all-out search for the truth sufficient for survival is available. (War departments have their human resources research programmes. Why not do as much for peace?)

10. **Manpower Through Money Power** — 160

> The half-truth that peace cannot be bought must be challenged. Peace waging (no less than war waging) requires a division of labour and this division of labour, no less than any other, necessitates an adequate use of the medium of exchange.

11. **Individual and Group Action** — 172

> Peace action, including research action, cannot take place unless individuals *act* and *act co-operatively*. Pertinent behaviour on the part of a few 'common men of uncommon courage' in each of many communities could generate dynamic nuclei of humanistic and scientific sanity. Such grass-roots groups, if suitably designed and adequately 'advertised', could add up to a World Wide Society for the Promotion of a Science of Peace.

12. **Résumé** — 185

> This world needs nothing so immediately as the elimination of war. For this we lack necessary and adequate understanding. Intelligent and serious and organized search for this knowledge is our greatest imperative. Helping to provide a new division of labour for this search can become the opportunity of any concerned person anywhere in the world.

Postscript to Second Printing — 194

I

THE SETTING—MANKIND AT THE CROSSROADS

THERE is still a chance for the human race to reach a most unbelievably happy tomorrow. The dynamic surge of a scientific civilization promises to relieve man of the handicaps of ignorance and poverty and disease. This in turn may release man's artistic creativity at a level thus far unimaginable. We seem to be moving with increasing speed toward a new worldwide golden age. This, however, is only one of the two highly contrasted possibilities.

There is extreme danger that the road we now travel will suddenly carry us over the cliff and into an abyss from which it would require centuries to recover, if ever. Amidst the dreams and hopes and promises of one world, we face the possibility of no world at all. The creative genius of man has fostered a towering structure of technology now threatened with cataclysmic collapse. Civilization seems to hang in the balance, sick and ill-suited to choose between sanity and suicide.

The danger which surrounds us has no parallel. Never before has there been the combination of so intense a display of hostility coupled with organization for antagonism on such a large scale, implemented with such powerful instruments of destruction. Huge aggregations of human beings numbering hundreds of millions are vigorously engaged in circumventing, containing, frustrating, and threatening to annihilate each other. Science and education and the arts of organization and communication are enlisted as never before in nihilistic preparation. Men appear attitudinally unsuited to negotiate this crisis. They who live in a fool's paradise have no patience for a Jeremiah who might disturb their sleep. Too few seem disposed to take the time to search out a point of view which is at once optimistic and realistic. The inertia and apparent indifference of so many men who are about to die is perhaps the most alarming feature in this most critical situation.

Our danger is progressive. We move with unprecedented speed

toward disaster of unprecedented proportions. No thoughtful and informed person can assume that the destructiveness of World War III would be at the same level as that of World War II. The latter destroyed tens of millions of lives and hundreds of billions of dollars worth of material goods. World War III, if it comes, would likely destroy hundreds of millions of lives and leave the remainder of the world's population almost wholly devoid of material goods and resources. Physical science seems only to have begun to show the capacity of human intelligence to develop tools of unlimited destruction. The longer the postponement of World War III, the more terrible its devastation when and if it comes. (Therefore, our urgent need for a profound solution—one suited not merely to postpone but to eradicate war.)

The paradox of human contradiction has reached an all-time high. With well-nigh universal desire to live, men seem to be making the most elaborate preparation to die. While sick of the sight of slaughter and misery and despair thus far produced by war, the nations of the earth are making their most prodigious preparations for ever greater war. At the stage of man's greatest 'enlightenment' and 'humanitarianism' the foremost nations of our time pile higher and higher their stock of tools for destruction. This we do for the sake of 'security' and with an assumption of sanity. With the conquest of hunger and disease only partially completed, the resources of the earth are being wasted in human conflict. Behold human ingenuity increasingly dedicated to human frustration and destruction.

All this activity is distinctly human. All the parts of the process which speed us on our downward drift consist of actions resulting from human decision. Nothing in man's extra-social environment forces him to do this. The cause of man's trouble is man—volitional man.

However, individual responsible minds do not deliberately and consciously strive to bring on the overall impending resultant event of cultural and racial suicide. The termination of the human race or of civilization is not the deliberate conscious purpose of any person or group of persons. If we go on and destroy ourselves, it will be by way of inadvertence and indirection. If the dark possibilities eventuate, it will happen because each individual, living by his accustomed motives of personal security and advancement, has contributed to the slaughter of the mass of which he is a part. Nations bent on preserving their sovereignty and honour will have extinguished each other. Thus they will have destroyed, without having intended to do so, the race; or at least, the civilization which makes national and individual advancement possible.

As surely as war is increasing, man's chances of survival are decreasing. There seems only one alternative to eventual extinction of man by war: namely, the extinction of war by man. As long as the expanding business and art and science of armament continues, man's assumption of continued survival is false. It is the height of folly to trust our destiny to the daily skill of diplomats in an armed world camp full of tension and misunderstanding. The use of our time and intelligence and emotion to fix moral and political blame in a world devoid of adequate moral coherence and adequate political technology is pragmatically stupid. It is false to assume that because war and civilization have coexisted in the past they therefore can do so in the future. Pre-atomic and atomic war are not the same. The choice between war and extinction versus peace and survival becomes daily more urgent.

Although this societal disease called war is widely recognized no widely accepted cure has been discovered. The author of this book wishes to present a working hypothesis for organizing a strenuous search for an acceptable solution. Our acute present situation has arisen out of a chronic situation which has been going on for two or three centuries or more. The tragic feature in this situation is the process of high acceleration in growth of physical power without comparable and adequate growth in social harmony. The crucial factor in this unbalanced process is the misuse of human intelligence—the misordering of science. The remedy is to be found through rapid redirection of man's intellectual energies—the reordering of scientific enterprise. This distinctly calls for no flight from reason and reality. Our justifiable prejudices against the science of the past must be faced. Our unjustified prejudices against the science of the future must be corrected. This is no time for anything slower than what Pavlov referred to as 'the all-powerful method of science'. It is now in order to develop a philosophy of thought and action, of reason and emotion, in which we can hope to save ourselves; not in spite of science, but *by* science.

A new and more adequate faith in peace and harmony, through love and reason, is required. To save ourselves from self-destruction, we have what it takes. We have untapped resources for co-operation and goodwill. We have the potential mentality to devise the method to find the know-how for harmonizing the purposes of individuals and of nations. We seem to have overlooked the possibility of combining, into one spirit, scientific and humanistic attitudes. To further the recognition of this amazing opportunity is the purpose of this book.

Perspective and Definition

Before continuing our diagnosis of the sickness of modern society let us orient our viewpoint and define a few terms used in this book.

BEYOND THE PROBLEM OF PEACE AND WAR

While this treatise is specifically concerned with the immediate problem of inter-nation peace we wish now to take time to indicate that the proposed science of peace is but a first, though indispensable first, step towards a science of man or a science of human culture. It is essential to such a science of man for two reasons. First, unless the science of peace enables us to find the road to survival there will be no culture in which to carry on a science of culture or there even may be no men left to carry on such an enterprise. In the second place, so far as can be anticipated now, it is safe to say that the discoveries which will enable us to eradicate war will include some of the discoveries essential to the guidance of cultural evolution beyond the time when war threatens our cultural and human existence. Harmony among the nations is a part of the larger harmony including relations among individuals and other groups now in existence as well as those to come. It may even include, or overlap with, discoveries essential to peace or harmony within the individual personality. It may also have much to do with the forward thrust of numerous cultural enterprises long frustrated and in doubt, such as the artistic and religious. Any contribution to a science of peace is a contribution to a science of human happiness. The true alternative to war and extinction is not survival in a slightly modified *status quo*. The true alternative is life at a higher standard—a higher standard of economic life, of aesthetic life, of social life, of intellectual life.

DEFINITION OF PEACE

An essential aspect of the outlook presented in this manuscript is that the full knowledge of what peace is can come only as our culture progresses, which in turn can come only as further progress is made in our mental conquest of the unknown. Certain aspects, however, need now to be pinned down.

1. A peaceful world is a warless world. However much we may cavil at the negativity involved in the conception of peace as the absence of war, we cannot escape the proposition that while and where there is war there is not peace.

2. The conception of war must include the phenomenon of war preparation. The illusion of peace between wars must be rigorously avoided. One of the requisites of peace is that nations cease arming. A somewhat unpopular way to say this is that peace among the nations eventually necessitates disarmament of the nations—all the nations. Getting ready is, today, a very vital part of the war process. The point of view throughout this book is that peace and total elimination of the institution of war are highly synonymous terms.

3. As a supplement to the statement that peace is the absence of war (including war preparation) we submit the converse, that war is the absence of peace. Peace is a process. War is the absence of the processes which are unifying from the point of view of all the nations of the world. What these processes are—finding them out—is the job of the science of peace. This presents a positive goal for thinkers and scholars and researchers concerned with man's cultural destiny. Stated bluntly and simply, the positive opportunity is to ascertain not what causes war, but what can cause peace. We need to discover what are and what can become the unifying processes in worldwide human relations.

4. This necessitates the wholeistic human point of view. Intra-national harmony including intra-national loyalties can serve only to aggravate the threat to our culture and our race as long as the conflict and the antagonisms between the nations or the nation blocs grow more intense. An increased emphasis upon brotherhood at the world level is essential. It is a dangerous assumption which says let harmony begin at home—that peace

at the lower levels is the best and the safest and the shortest route to harmony among the nations. The burden of proof of whatever truth there be in this general assumption must be put upon those who hold to it. (Whenever the pronoun we is used—non-editorially—in this book it refers to *we humans*.)

DEFINITION OF SCIENCE AND SCIENCE OF PEACE

The concept of science is discussed at great length in Chapters 5, 6, and 7. Throughout these chapters the reader will be challenged to a judicious and perhaps new emphasis upon various aspects of the total complex concept of science. One warning here is not to think of science exclusively or primarily as *knowledge* but rather as search or *research for knowledge* and understanding. The characteristics of such serious or systematic search, referred to as scentific method, are combined in somewhat different patterns for research in different areas. Rigid and highly limited conception of science is partly responsible for the tragic delay in the growth of science of human relations. Science is a process for solving problems through improved understanding, through new facts and ideas, and new combinations of facts and ideas.

Let us think of peace science as a process—an intellectual process in which a considerable number of fearless and free individuals devote their time and utmost capabilities to an objective and co-operative and creative search for those knowledges which will give men the enlightenment necessary to implement whatever honest desire they possess for a harmonious and warless world. This creative, co-operative, objective, relentless search must not omit careful and systematic observation of and study of the subjective or emotional factors involved in human relations. It must include the utmost study of human attitudes insofar as they are found to be essential factors in the phenomenon of peace and war.

REGARD FOR THE PRINCIPLE OF DIVISION OF LABOUR

We believe there is considerable confusion in the minds of most people in the crucial matter of assuming responsibility for the elimination of war. Here again much of our judgment must be suspended. The point of view, however, in this manuscript does not stress the oft-repeated phrase *'Every person must do his share'*. The problem is not to get everyone to do his share, but to get enough people to take enough of a share soon enough to get the job done. The scientific part of the struggle for peace need not be universal, but those who struggle must struggle universally (i.e., in a spirit of universal concern). We cannot expect everybody to do everything. The science of peace cannot come alive unless and until we actively recognize the principle of *division of labour*.

Whatever exceptions there may be to this principle in the final act of the drama of putting an end to human warfare, there can be no doubt about those early phases in which the essential task is to search and discover the knowledges necessary for effective understanding, i.e., the research part of the enterprise. Scientific research requires extreme and special expertness and it cannot succeed except through the instrumentation of experts or specialists. It requires men of extraordinary experience—men who treat it as a special problem and who give to it special and extraordinary attention. Even if the task should require the full time of a million men this would constitute less than one-tenth of one per cent of the world's population. Of course the percentage needed to furnish the necessary moral and financial support will eventually be much greater.

The question now is not who will be among the last to furnish this support but who will be among the first. The goal of this treatise is to help stimulate this pioneer support—enough support to inaugurate a chain reaction of research for the understanding necessary to save our culture from collapse and our race from extinction.

This need for a new division of labour will be injected repeatedly in our discussion. Let us now resume our tentative diagnosis in the next four chapters.

2
A CRISIS IN CULTURE

OUR warfare world is a world of men. The destruction being prepared is being prepared by men. *Why?* Why do men prepare a fate so undesired? How can we most hopefully and honestly analyse this unbelievably tragic situation? Assuming that there is no direct instinct for self destruction, is there any realistic way to understand this puzzling performance of the human species?

An enormous amount of research is required to resolve this challenging enigma. In this and the two succeeding chapters is presented a sort of preliminary and hypothetical diagnosis of our current baffling situation. This is for the purpose of indicating three general directions which our thinking may well take for achieving a comprehensive grip upon our problem. Our threefold suggestion is that we look to our misdirected though rapidly evolving culture, to our social misorganization, and to the misorder in our application of scientific intelligence. This chapter takes note of the general role of culture in the behaviour of men.

Man as individual and as species is in the clutch of the culture[1] which happens to have evolved. We (billions of humans of this generation) are suffering from unfortunate ways of behaving—

---

[1] The term culture is here used in a *very* broad sense. In the first place we are not referring to a single separate culture such as the culture of certain European or Asian or African or Australian peoples, but the total complex of cultures of all men at the present time—including all sections and subsections and all currents and cross currents. We will later point out that the cross currents and contradictions in the total culture constitute appalling attributes of modern life. Also let us emphasize that culture as here used includes all our present ways of behaving not posssessed by Cro-Magnon man 50 or 100 thousand years ago. It includes (a) our attitudes—values, beliefs, fears, prejudices, superstitions, loyalties, loves, and hates; (b) our institutions or organizations,—political, economic, industrial, religious, familial, social, etc.; (c) our tools or implements—ploughs, tractors, tanks, motorcars, trains, planes, guns, and guided missiles; (d) our knowledges and skills, including communication, language, literature, music, and painting. Also included is a vast and recent array of scientific facts and understandings about plants and animals, and about atoms and molecules and planets. Our array of facts greatly affects our attitudes and values and enables us to operate our complicated pattern of organizations and to devise and maintain and operate our marvellous kit of tools.

ways of feeling, thinking and acting. Some of these ways are excellent and admirable. Some are harmless, but some are unsuited to the rest of the pattern. For instance, knowledge and technology for making hydrogen bombs does not go well with strong and unqualified patriotism towards nations of unlimited sovereignty. We are, in a twofold sense, the creatures of habit. The behaviour of each individual is greatly controlled by his own habits and by the habits of others.

The behaviour of the individual varies with the variation of the culture. Let us look at one of the more obvious types of influences —that of the tools. Note what one cannot do before certain tools are invented. Christopher Columbus was *not* privileged to pilot the *Queen Mary* across the Atlantic, *nor* to make an Atlantic crossing in an air-conditioned stratospheric plane or anticipate objects of obstruction by radar, or to radio news of his landing in the West Indies to his friends in Europe. Three and a half centuries later, one of his beneficiaries swinging his cradle in an Ohio wheatfield was scarcely privileged to dream of a tractor-drawn combine which would cut and thrash his wheat at one operation a hundred times as fast. A century later the great-great-grandson of our nineteenth-century wheat-grower, working in a combine and tractor factory in Chicago, may or may not wish for the open-air life of his great-great-grandfather, but whether he likes it or not the changing culture has diminished the number who can make a living in the open air. It has also increased the number who spend their time in factories making cars and tractors, etc., i.e., using tools to make tools. Said descendant may not care to live in the open air. The cultural change has changed man's options and his preferences. Not only have the tools changed but social organization has changed greatly. Mammoth governments and industrial corporations and great ecclesiastical and educational bodies set the stage and tend to fix the range of individual or personal choices. The culture sets limits to the freedom of thought, including freedom of belief and of learning. An individual who believed in witchcraft likely lived in a community where witches were burned. Sun-worshippers live among sun-worshippers. Christians, Moslems, Buddhists, tend to be the children of Christians, Moslems, Buddhists. Renegades are relatively rare. Subversionists are punished. So it is with other aspects of our character. Our fears and hopes, our tolerances and antipathies and our moral convictions have their origin in the culture about us. So it is with our knowledges. For the most part the facts we possess are social property. The data in a million books are in a sense accessible to millions of individuals any one of whom in a lifetime could not have accumulated by original research as much as one thousandth of one per cent thereof. Each average-sized adult head carries around with it tens of thousands of ideas and bits of information which in one way or another have been acquired through direct or indirect contact with other contemporary heads. But whether we think of the pages of books and documents or of the grey matter in human heads, there is a limit to the contents of this encyclopaedic well or reservoir; and the life of the individual is conditioned by what the reservoir does and does not contain. For instance, as long as the well contains knowledge for hydrogen warfare but not knowledge sufficient for internation peace, the individual will be likely to live a dangerous and dreadful life natural to a citizen in a warfare world, as over against the life appropriate to a citizen in a world at peace.

The individual is beneficiary and victim of a culture which for the most part he did not create. Much of it has been fashioned and bequeathed to him by hundreds of previous generations. It is maintained by hundreds of millions of his contemporaries. It is the net resultant from trillions of decisions by billions of minds operating through millions of public and private crises. His inheritance is a great culture—daily growing greater under the impact of world-wide communication resulting in cosmopolitan education and intellectual cross-fertilization. It has often been remarked that the world has grown smaller. In an important sense, however, the world of the individual has become vastly larger. For each of us the cultural environment has become far more extensive and far more complex. The number of living persons upon whom and from whom the individual exerts and receives pressure in our modern world is enormous. The total ocean of humanity in which we wallow contains literally billions. Increasingly each individual shares the privileges and responsibilities of his ongoing culture with a billion or more other culture-bound earthlings. His freedom might almost be compared with the freedom of a drop of water in the Pacific Ocean.

Since a man is so greatly a creature of his culture why does he take so little responsibility for his culture and the destiny or direction of its evolution? One answer is—because the culture is so big and he is so little. The weight of his individual influence is so tiny along side the massive momentum with which the culture moves. Out of this sinister fact idealistic impulses are born and buried by the millions daily. Very often and very naturally the individual is driven back upon himself to attempt not to save his culture but to save himself from his culture. In his frustration the individual seems to say, 'The world must look after itself. I cannot be its keeper. Charity must begin at home'. The slogan, 'The Lord helps *those* who help *themselves*', comes to sound more and more like 'The Lord helps *him* who helps *himself*'.

This abnormality of practical individualism seems to be accentuated by a very frequent escape mechanism which says that there are other persons who are not helpless, who have real freedom and social opportunity, and that the responsibility for social improvement rests upon these *other* persons. Is it not true, however, that so-called leaders are as truly in the grip of the culture as are the so-called followers? He who gets too far beyond his culture is not likely to become 'Prime Minister' and if he does he is not likely to remain so. There is a strong tendency for potential saviours of human culture to meet with crucifixion. The smallness of any one individual in comparison with the massiveness of the culture makes reasonable the position that the single individual is no match for the inertia or momentum of the mass of culture-bound individuals who constitute our great society.

One very serious feature of present-day thought and feeling is our lack of faith in one another. The race seems to lack faith in itself. The species suffers low reputation in the mind of its members. The notion has leaked out that 'people are no "damned" good', and that our present culture is the best of all possible cultures, human nature being what it is. No greater error can be found than in the general assumption so often unconsciously made that the human race is necessarily as bad and unfit as its present cultural expression—that it is incapable of a better culture. This misappraisal of our cultural possibilities is one of the most serious defects in our current culture.

Let us take heart. A new line of cultural evolution seems to be opening up. This might be referred to as culture self-criticism. The concept of culture is new. The notion of cultural evolution still finds serious obstacles in the belief or value system of many groups. The race has only begun to become culture-conscious. Bold and constructive criticism of our overall culture is overdue.

Let us now take time for a general two-point criticism. Two of the most outstanding criticisms which can be levelled at the totality of modern culture are that it lacks unity, and that it lacks balance or proportion. We wish here to sketch these only briefly, as they will be dealt with in greater detail in two succeeding chapters. These criticisms deal frankly with the negative features in the picture. They are stressed because in spite of all the positive features which can be mentioned these negative features are capable of bringing a sudden and tragic end to our great and amazing era of progress.

The Lack of Unity

Unity or harmony, though not the only need of our culture, surely is one of the greatest. Probably unity, or whatever it is that is required for greater unity or harmony, is at this point the most basic and urgent of all our cultural needs. The culture is divisive. It pits man against man. Organizations stand out against organizations, groups against groups. This for long has made it a wasteful and inefficient culture. More and more it threatens to make it an extinct culture. We become more and more capable of mass production of massive tools of destruction. Daily our factories become more enormous. More and more we operate these to make the tools to destroy the factories for making tools. Parallel with this, moreover, our culture shows more and more capacity for the mass production of mass fears. Much of this latter, though inseparable from our massive tools of destruction, are a function of that other part or subdivision of our culture previously referred to as attitude—values, ideologies, beliefs. Here we behold the most amazing array of intellectual contradictions— moral division and confusion. Heretofore we have consented to this under conditions which are passing and hence make further consent and acquiescence more and more irrational and dangerous. We have consented not because the division and the contradictions are good in and of themselves, but because the known alternatives of violence and intellectual and political tyranny are even more irrational and unacceptable. Too often these contradictions and irrationalities have been condoned in the interest of intellectual stimulation. More and more as both religious and political curtains are drawn between conflicting groups and conflicting ideologies, these differences have proved stultifying and disintegrating rather than stimulating. Most of all our tolerating and condoning and even extolling has come because of a lack of a practicable procedure for dealing with these immense contradictions. It is a sobering fact that these conflicts in our values and ideas are often so deep that men speak seriously of dying, literally, for their faith.

Both geographically and sociologically viewed, ours is a strikingly uneven culture. Both within and between communities and sections of the globe we find wealth and poverty, literacy and illiteracy, health and disease side by side. More and more this is a function, not of the necessities or accidents of the physical environment but of the culture causation or accident.

Much of the conflict and contradiction among our values is defended in the name of diversity. This we believe is false. The great challenge to our culture-ology is to find the secret of combining a far greater unity with a far greater diversity and freedom. Diversity must be respected and increased—conflict must be cured or at least diminished. The fact that modern man has become so greatly organized and has concurrently lost so much freedom suggests, as we shall point out in the next chapter, that man the organizer too often has gotten off on the wrong foot. Therefore we must seek with greater vigilance and better methods a new and better pattern of organization. Let us have courage. Unity has shown great possibilities of growth even though there are manifest weaknesses and appalling dangers creeping into the overall process. Greater cultural unity seems now inevitable providing we can forestall certain portentous types of collapse.

Our Culture Out of Proportion

Our second general diagnosis says that an unbalanced development has given us, if not the accentuation of our conflict, at least intolerable danger from our conflict. Our cultural state might be compared to an organic or biological monster whose organs are out of proportion and incapable of efficient working relationship. We are too long on some things considering our shortness on others. Let us say it in reverse if we wish, but the fact of disproportion must not be dodged. The major features of this imbalance have been variously phrased—the cultural lag—man's internal progress too slow for man's external progress—a too materialistic culture—man's physical satisfactions ahead of his social satisfactions—an advanced mechanical or physical technology alongside of a retarded social technology—physical tools extremely powerful with social tools or methods extremely uncertain. In Chapter 4 we will indicate our preference for describing this situation as *physical power increase, too much too fast too soon*, and *social harmony increase, too little too slow too late*. For instance, man's ancient dream of flying has come true very suddenly, but his dream of world peace is dangerously delayed.

By the accident of our culture and the lack of overall guidance of its evolution, knowledge and understanding of physical relations has outrun our knowledge and understanding of human relations. Our present knowledge for making powerful tools is extensive and effective. Progress in our knowledge for improving human character is in great question. That this disproportionate search for these two kinds of knowledge continues increasingly in spite of the increasing evidence against it, is one of the darkest aspects of our diagnosis. A better culture is needed—a more unified and balanced culture—a culture with a better and more complete set of tools and techniques, with better and more positive and unifiying beliefs and feelings, with better and more appropriate pattern of organization, and with better knowledges and understandings. But can this be achieved?

Is a Better Culture Possible?

In view of certain considerations it would be illogical to set any limits to the range of future cultural possibilities, i.e., if civilization does not explode and collapse. First, let us consider how unreasonable to assume a static view of culture. Our current culture is nothing if not incomplete. Is it not logical to believe that the best songs have not yet been sung? The best tools not yet invented? The best knowledge not yet discovered? The highest wisdom not yet attained? (That is, if the culture and the race do not come to an untimely end through self destruction.) Creative and dynamic qualities of our modern culture are very great. The present hour is no time to fear cultural stagnation. (Barring extreme dangers of tyranny and war.) The rapidity of change in certain aspects constitutes a considerable hazard. Our legitimate fear is that our changes will move us in directions suited to cultural collapse. We say 'rapidity of change in certain aspects'. One of our dangers is that men will cling too long to values whose survival function is no longer adequate. Old moral and ethical concepts useful in yesterday's culture may not prove well suited to new levels of knowledge and speed and power.

Another occasion for optimism is in the observation of the element of accident up to now. Why be surprised that the accidents of cultural evolution should turn out no better than they have? The wonder is that our culture has so much good in it. The culturologists of the present and the future can help us determine how certain cultural changes have come to take place in certain directions and not in others. For purposes of our discussion here, it is important to note that some tools have been invented and others not, some creeds have been formulated, and not others, some institutions have been organized and not others, some facts have been discovered and not others. No one can now tell with completeness and clarity the nature, form, and substance or content of these uninvented tools, unformulated creeds, unorganized institutions, and undiscovered knowledge. But this is no logical support to the assumption that what has happened is the only thing that could have happened. In this connection there seems only one defensible position, namely, our present complex culture is neither as bad nor as good as it might have been. *It might have been different.*

A very strong support for potential multidirectionality of culture change is found in the great variety existing among the separate cultures thus far developed throughout the world. While Mediterranean and Eastern cultures were developing a civilization on wheels, the Mayan culture in America was developing one without wheels. This is only one of a vast number of contrasts.

Let us now take up another term and note that the evolution or development of our culture has been unguided. Like biological evolution, up to now cultural evolution had to find its way as best it could under the impact of the blind forces of nature. The fact that the human part of the nature has played such a major role does not alter the fact that we have had an enormous amount of change without a master design for it to follow. Of course the one great differential between mammals and man—intelligence—

has been the crucial factor in human cultural development. This intelligence has indispensably functioned to propel. It did not guide. It was not used in the interest of an over-all design. There has been no long-range principle to guide the application of intelligence. The total design or destiny was left to chance. A guided culture could surely evolve not only at a steeper rate but in safer directions.

Human Intelligence as a Guide for Human Culture

The only agent for conscious cultural improvement is man—rational man. Only a sincere use of our intelligence can save us. There is no substitute. This ununified, imbalanced trend, this dynamic, incomplete, unguided evolution and its threat of collapse is a tremendous challenge to our highest mental processes. The impulse to dream of utopia is not new, but these dreams have never had the blessing of an adequate, appropriate amount of careful, systematic, unrelenting study. Since human intelligence has gotten us into the present mess why not use it to get us out? Why not use our reason to turn the threat of cultural collapse into an opportunity to move on to a higher ground?

Intelligently guided, cultural evolution is the true antidote for cultural revolutionary collapse. Through courageous effort we can thus work out a beneficent compromise twixt conservatism and radicalism. A safe and sound cultural progress requires democratic guidance. This in turn can come only from enlightenment and understanding based upon more adequate knowledge. This knowledge can come only through research. If this means a prodigious amount of research, let us not flinch. The stakes are high. We have made a start in some of the anthropology and some of the other social science which has studied at the descriptive level a number of the separate cultures. It should not be difficult to go ahead and study the over-all culture.

Roughly speaking, the research will eventually have to make good on at least three points: first, the desirable cultural goals or directions; second, the means of reaching a particular goal or effecting a given redirection; third, technique or procedure for achieving democratic agreement regarding both the goals and the means. In the determination of our cultural goals or directions we will have to dare to make comparisons and preferential judgments among rival alternatives. For this purpose objective criteria will be needed. Preliminarily we can probably agree on the general characteristics of greater unity and greater balance and a lessened danger of explosion and collapse. Other and implementary goals or subgoals can doubtless be developed as we devote a reasonably appropriate amount of serious attention to the task.

As to the means of achieving new cultural goals, perhaps we have made a beginning in the process of deliberate association and re-association of individuals into new groups and of old and new groups into new and larger associations. Let not our present stalemates daunt us. If it be argued that the League of Nations failed and that the United Nations is still weak and ineffective it should be remembered that two unsuccessful attempts at such a level give no true occasion for surrender, since the amount of intelligence and other resources thus far invested have been such a very small fraction of the total possible.

The deliberate changing of the current of a culture is of course a task of enormous magnitude. But what better investment is there for human imagination and reason? The utopias of the past have tended too much to be the dreams of single and separate individuals. The utopias of the future should not be confused with these nor with the unhappy attempts of despotic individuals, however beneficent. The temptation to tyranny is one of our great hazards. A democratic science and technology of culture deserves to rate a high place in a comprehensive and legitimate division of labour. In general acceptance and in social support such a new division of labour can become a dynamic new dimension of our culture.

Summary

World culture is dangerously defective. An accidental culture is unreliable. A better culture is possible. A guided culture is demanded. While single and separate individuals are powerless to change the currents of their culture, there is great power and possibility of choice left to men collectively if they can effect adequate and appropriate organization.

Recommendations

1. We must face the music fearlessly. If we have to point out great defects in our education or our religion, our economics or

our politics, let it be remembered that our first business is not to compliment ourselves. We are living in a dangerous age. Our culture is critically ill. Finding the cure requires our willingness to criticize any aspect of it.

2. We must be positive. The cure must be creative. We must not be merely able to point out what is actively wrong but what is missing. Very probably the errors of commission are not as serious or subtle or as likely to be overlooked as our errors of omission. The most serious thing probably is not what someone is doing, but in something that no one is doing.

3. Let us constantly remind each other of the need to discover, nurture, and maintain a broad social viewpoint. A nationalistic or other subcultural viewpoint is not adequate in a global setting. A non-partisan viewpoint is indispensable. The point of view must not be American, Asian, or African. It must be human—wholeisticly human.

4. Let us be responsible. Let us avoid the almost universal tendency to shift the blame for our social ills to other groups within our nation or to other individuals within a group. We cannot afford the costly luxury of yielding to the insidious temptation to mutual denunciation. This widespread tendency is very natural for any individual or group as it strives for ego defence and competitive and comparative self-respect. Every inch we yield, however, to this temptation adds to the defilement of our hearts and the confusion of our heads. For centuries philosophers have deplored this trait. In the atomic age it may prove fatal. To overcome this tendency not to accept responsibility for oneself or one's group is no easy matter. It is one of the deepest grooves of cultural habit.

5. Let us emphasize our collective strength. Let us no longer frustrate ourselves with a false idealism which overrates the present extent of freedom and amount of independence of the individual. But let us substitute for this a much overdue enthusiasm for the freedom of collective man and the possibilities of unlimited progress for the human species as we achieve corporate unity. The culture need not collapse. Men need not become paralysed with fear. The promise of tomorrow, however, is ours only if we claim it collectively. This calls for special emphasis upon the problem of how to organize ourselves for greater unity.

3
SOCIETY MISORGANIZED

THIS chapter attempts to bring into sharper focus the institutional or organizational aspects of our present-day world cultural crisis. The previous statement that man is beneficiary and victim of his culture now becomes: man is beneficiary and victim of his institutions. In order to defend the sanity of the individual we here introduce the concept of the insanity or sickness of society. This sickness need not be fatal. We are capable of better organization.

HIGH LEVEL ORGANIZATION OF SOCIETY

Modern man is highly organized. Long ago, Aristotle pointed out that man is a political animal. This can be taken as a brief way of saying that man is an organizing and organizable animal. Over a period of time, he has hit upon numerous and complicated procedures for negotiating his social environment. Often he has been successful in his effort to simplify his interpersonal and intergroup relations. However, the total pattern has grown more complex. Social issues have multiplied and become more confusing.

A careful discussion and description of all aspects and instances of this phenomenon of organization would fill many an encyclopaedia. Let us call attention to a few outstanding features of modern organization. One of the striking observations is the enormous size of a great many of our institutions. A hundred thousand families may achieve their livelihood as employees of a single corporation, which in turn and in part serves some of the needs of each of millions of families. A hundred million persons may trust to a single government for their economic and physical security. We also attempt to serve our educational needs and satisfy our religious wants through organizations vast and numerous and highly interacting and interlocked with each other and with our political and industrial bodies.

In all this ramified pattern of institutionality, we observe a twofold multiplicity. On the one hand, each institution affects a great many individuals; on the other hand, each individual is affected by a great many institutions. This is significant with regard to two things we have said about the individual, namely, his helplessness and his confusion. If an individual is to control his destiny, he has to participate in the control of a great many institutions. To affect an institution, he has somehow to achieve unity of action with a great many persons. Institutional betterment cannot be achieved as a solitary fact by a single individual. Democratic modification of an institution results from common purpose consciously and co-ordinately pursued. But how can this be done unless each individual achieves some insight into the purposes and intentions of a great many other persons?

Social Misorganization

In all our institutional activity, we are only partially effective in expressing our wants, in achieving our needs. An organized institution might be defined as a more or less successful mechanism and technique for human co-ordination and co-operation. It is often said that any institution will survive only as long as it serves a real need. This, we believe, can be a dangerous partial statement of the truth. Institutions are supported not merely in terms of how well they serve us, but in terms of how well we believe them to serve us and what we believe to be the possibilities and impossibilities of more desirable alternatives. By virtue of a kind of momentum and a type of rigidity, institutions can persist long after their total and net effect upon human welfare is reduced to zero or less.

In our present organizational impasse we have one of the greatest ironies of all time. We have made great effort to solve the problems of human relations through human organization. But our problems grow constantly greater. To many they appear more and more insoluble. To protect their freedom and to achieve increased satisfaction individuals organize. Often they find, however, that their freedom has shrunk and their hopes are frustrated. We have developed more and more institutions of ever greater size to make life more worth the living. These same institutions in their total pattern and net effect threaten more and more to destroy our civilization and possibly all life. In the end our devices for improving life may result in life's elimination. This sinister fact of inadequate organization too often escapes our attention because the total picture is one of great mixture. The total pattern of social relationship includes almost innumerable instances of effective co-operation through indispensable association. Looked at piecemeal, there seems to be a wealth of evidence that we are highly successful at organization. The net result of the total pattern, however, is appalling.

To the extent that our institutions enable us to achieve our maximum satisfactions and to reduce to a minimum our frustrations, we are well organized. To whatever extent they do not thus enable us to achieve our maximum potential, as set by our physical environment and by our physical, intellectual and emotional nature, we are misorganized.

The earth on which we dwell has much highly suitable climate and fertile soil. Our potential resources make it possible for us to be well fed and comfortably clothed, sheltered, and generally healthy and energetic. In so far as this is prevented by unsuitable economic arrangements, we can say we are ill-organized. Let us illustrate with two types of conditions.

First, note the great depression in the thirties. This affected considerable portions of the earth and, in turn, seems to have made considerable contribution toward the hastening of World War II. In places where there was no crop failure and no shortage of mineral and other natural resources, there was still deprivation. In a city where shoe leather was abundant, machinery and men were idle, and children were without shoes. Some said it was over-production; some said it was under-consumption. More and more we got around to saying that our processes of 'distribution' were inadequate. The 'rich' blamed the 'poor'. The 'poor' blamed the 'rich'. From all this, one might conclude that people are not fit to associate with people. A more constructive generalization, however, could well be that while people are not perfect, they could live more satisfactorily if they could be better organized.

But let us take a wider illustration of the so-called problem of distribution. The world has become familiar with the spectacle of famine concurrent with a surplus of food. Famine in the absence of food could be charged up to our inability to negotiate adequately our physical environment. But in our time, what do we witness? Famine that starves and stints and kills goes on in certain areas of the earth. At the same time in other areas of the same world, food that is surplus grows stale and even rots. This is not the fault of our physical environment. It is our ineptness with our social environment.

Since often this coincidental food and famine is separated by oceans, we tend to overlook and accept the facts as inevitable. 'Suppose it is true that in Asia people are cursed with poverty and starvation while in the U.S.A. they are dismayed with surpluses of "over-production". Are not oceans and mountains barriers to transportation?' The answer is 'No'.

The barriers are in our heads and hearts. They are in our habits of social behaviour. Physically, we have conquered these mountains and oceans. This we have demonstrated not only by the food and other legitimate cargoes we carry on occasion. We have ironically demonstrated this physical victory by the cargoes of destruction we have been sending and anticipate sending from one side of the world to the other. Our distributional incompetence is not physical.

But our ineptness at distributing food is not all. We do not have the best possible arrangement for maximal goodwill and trust. If we have it within us to be peaceful and law-abiding, and our processes of government and education do not bring this out, we can say we are politically and educationally ill-organized. We live at a time when men prepare desperately for a war that no one intrinsically wants.

The fears which threaten to wreck us are fears which relate to no lack of control over the physical environment. Neither can they be put down as an absolute necessity of human nature. They relate to our lack of control over our social institutions. They are fostered by the unfortunate drift in the total pattern of human organization.

Criterion for Misorganization—Co-operation for Antagonism

If we are to save ourselves from consummate destruction, we must help social evolution to take a new direction. If human intelligence is to function maximally in this guidance of organizational evolution, it will need to be guided by adequate criteria for differentiating the good from the bad—the better from the worse in human organization. For this we wish to suggest the following generalization. *We misorganize when we organize to antagonize one another.*

We suggest that co-operation be the key concept in organization. To the extent that institutions facilitate co-operation, we are well organized. To the extent that they foster antagonism among us as individuals or groups, we are misorganized. We are misorganized to the extent that we co-operate to antagonize or oppose.

The co-operative aspect (as well as other aspects) of the behaviour of any individual is qualified by the quality of his behavioural goal. A man's goals determine when he will co-operate, with whom he will co-operate, how he will co-operate, and with what outcome. Here we come face to face with the fact of conflict of goals. In all instances where men co-operate, they do so to achieve some common goal or end. Unfortunately, the goal common to some men may be contradictory to the goal common to others. Thus the goals common to some of us are the defeat and frustration of the goals of some others of us. Naturally then, but unfortunately, we find ourselves co-operating with some to antagonize others. This feature of human behaviour is so common that we tend to accept it as inevitable. We tend to make a virtue of an assumed necessity and develop our idealisms of loyalty and heroism in connection with it. A common observation is that co-operation and social solidarity require a common enemy. Frequently, the assumption goes unchallenged that this 'indispensable' enemy has to be human.

However, the lamentable and challenging fact is this: men now are organized for mutual frustration. The joint activity of the members of an organized group *may* be purely co-operative, or it *may* involve the purpose to antagonize and frustrate. The group goals sought are sometimes purely constructive but not always. The common purpose of the members of an organized group often are to antagonize and overthrow another group. Our great threat is in our capacity to co-operate, and organize, in order to antagonize and disorganize and thwart others. This is the unholy motivational mixture which confuses the head and curses the heart of modern man. In one and the same enterprise, yes, in one and the same act, we find ourselves co-operating with some and antagonizing others. This means our efforts are contradictory. They are sure to be wasteful. They may become fatal. Human survival requires a sharp and rapid turn away from this trend of ever greater organization for more intense and hostile antagonism between men and men.[1]

Features of Misorganization

We wish now to point out more concretely the ways in which men are organized for mutual opposition and frustration and for mutual destruction. In order to simplify, we will discuss six features of organization. These more or less represent six classes of institutions—political, military, economic, educational, religious, and communicational. The interlocking of institutional operation between and within these classes is a matter of great importance. We have spoken about the helplessness of the individual since he is at the mercy of the mass of individuals and at the mercy of his mass institutions. But note now that the institutions are at the mercy of each other. The interlocking pattern makes it difficult and, to some extent, impossible for any institution to redirect itself independently of the others.

We wish again to remind the reader that this is a pathological diagnosis. We cannot here take time to present a balanced picture by listing all the fortunate features in our society. We are trying to get at the crux of our crisis. This discussion is written under the shadow of a threat of a devastating third world war. The writer feels that our institutions are good but not good enough. Worst of all they are not good enough to bring enough peace to ensure survival.

The picture here presented is coloured by the background of the writer whose experiences have been in the West, particularly U.S.A. An observer in Asia or Russia might state the same thesis of social misorganization in different terms. In pointing out our

[1] This threat of human extinction through the clash of two or more organized political and military Goliaths is the underlying concern of this treatise. We wish to acknowledge, however, that this is only one of two dire disasters which may come to humanity as a result of our failure at organization. Briefly put, the second threat is the loss of individual freedom. The seeds of tyranny are scattered throughout the soil of every country. Some proclivity for autocracy resides in almost all organization. There is of course no reason why we cannot achieve both freedom and survival. *Democratic* global unity is our legitimate goal. Our dual criterion needs to be co-operation without antagonism and co-ordination without coercion.

dangers we have in mind of course our more highly organized and industrialized and formally educated countries.

A. THE POLITICAL FEATURE

The key factor in our organizational difficulties today is political. It sets the stage for co-operative antagonism. It affects the functional disunity of mankind on the largest scale. It restricts the freedom of the individual most unabashedly and unapologetically.

Five aspects should be noted. First, note the growth in size and the increased proximity of our sovereign nations. Growth of civilization is highly correlated with the growth of nations or states. Due to physical science, oceans and mountains no longer separate them. Secondly, note the great intra-national unity, functionally speaking. The power that is concentrated and can be focused in a given direction is enormous. Behold the era of power politics become the era of total war. Third, note that the cohesion within nations or groups of nations tends to be bought at the price of hostility between nations or groups of nations. For instance, citizens in the U.S.A. find themselves unitedly and devoutly wishing for the political breakdown and other misfortunes to the strength of Russia, and vice versa.

Fourth, note the changed relation between the individual and the state. Note the see-saw relation between the sovereignty of the state and the sovereignty of the individual. What the one gains, the other often tends to lose. Theoretically this is desirable and inevitable. The individual surrenders certain freedoms in order to gain others. However, the net increase in freedom is everywhere in question. 'Slave labour camp' is an ugly phrase, but there are others—concentration camps and detention camps for those who are classed as subversives—induction centres for those to be trained to shoot and ordered to kill by the state. We may defend this in the name of political stability, but nonetheless personal freedom grows less and survival grows more doubtful.

Fifth, note the dominance of the political over other institutions: educational, religious, industrial, and military. Of course, these relationships are not static. Frequently, they are ambiguous and obscure. But if big business, or big religious or big military organizations come to dominate the state, or vice versa, the net effect upon the freedom of the individual and his ability to help himself is negative and unfortunate.

B. THE MILITARY FEATURE

The second major feature of our misorganization is the military. It ties so closely to the political that one hesitates to mention it separately. War without politics is impossible. But politics without war is required for human survival. Increasingly, the military tail wags the political dog. Through relation to state and school and industry, our military organizations play an increasingly greater role in the daily life of individual men. No other feature in the body of society is so analagous to cancerous growth in the physiological body of the individual.

Our military institutions are the most explicit expression and the ultimate implement of men's attitude of antagonism. They constitute an ever louder reminder that man's philosophy of universal brotherhood is still a voice surrounded by much bewilderment. For those who are complacent about our lack of social and moral and political progress, two aspects of military 'progress' may be emphasized. One is the amazing increase in military might. The other is the speed with which it is taking place. Some argue that the destructive and decimating power of uranium or hydrogen or bacteriological bombs may not be sufficient to extinguish civilization and to terminate the race. This may be true. But physical science shows terrible acceleration. The god of war has achieved a stranglehold upon science.

War has become the world's biggest business. Consider the size of the military budget. The U.S. government appropriation (for wars past, present, and future), for illustration, is nearly a third of the national income. Britain and the U.S.S.R spend comparable sums.

C. THE ECONOMIC FEATURE

This means that our economic institutions are deeply involved. There are here, as elsewhere, ugly facts which we hesitate to stress. But face we must the fact of affinity between the business of war and other business. Whether we admit it or not, our economic selves like war. Some like it hot, some like it cold, but in one subtle way or another sooner or later there is widespread interest in the tonic which war preparation gives to business. The reciprocity is profound. Business and industry are taxed to support armament. But armament furnishes business and industry with much of its business. This feature is not universally uniform, but the complete divorcement between war and economics can be achieved only when war is eliminated from human culture.

Our various institutions and types of institutions are interactively interlocked economically. In a sense, all institutions are economic institutions. Anything which an institution does or might do to shut off its chance to draw its economic breath will almost surely cause it to expire. Practically all institutions operate through paid workers. If the pay stops, the work stops. This factor not only limits the independence of the institution but reduces the freedom of the individual. This terrible fact pertains to men and women who work for all types of agencies—military, civil, public and private, profit and non-profit.

D. EDUCATIONAL INSTITUTIONS

Our rapidly expanding political and military institutions increasingly tend to affect the institutions of education. War preparation is more than munitional. While industrial agencies furnish the materials necessary for war, the educational agencies prepare the personnel. For the production and use of the paraphernalia of war, certain abilities are necessary. Development of these abilities is the role of the educator. These abilities may be specific to war such as military tactics or the technology of arms design, manufacture, and care. Or they may be general, as the development of mathematical ability so widely required in peaceful operations as well as indispensable to modern warfare. Most serious of all is the extent to which higher educational institutions in some countries are induced to channel intellect into those scientific avenues useful to the war effort. Again the economic factor plays its role. To secure governmental and other financial aid as well as draft exemption for their students, more and more, colleges and universities need to show that they are essential to the military might of the country in which they are situated. Their contribution to inter-nation goodwill is of minor 'practical' importance. To other agencies colleges are indebted for job opportunities which motivate tuition-paying students.

But war preparation is more than a matter of ability. It is also a matter of attitude. War requires the disposition to develop and apply the ability to make and use tools of war. Schools, along with churches and mass communication agencies, prepare the individual attitudinally (i.e., morally and spiritually) for whatever conflict may come up. The attitude of co-operating to antagonize requires two distinct components; we are right, they are wrong. Teachers suspected of favourable leanings toward the enemy state are excluded from the classroom. To illustrate: Communist-country youth associate with teachers who abhor western style democracy and all they believe about it; U.S. youth are taught by teachers who abhor communism and all they associate with it. This is but the modern and acute version of a long-standing educational blockade. Broad cultural appeal is blocked by intercultural prejudice and interpolitical antipathy. This divisive process is caused by and perpetuates a divided world. Of course, there is the precedent of teacher and student international exchange. This seems qualitatively correct. Quantitatively, it is absurdly inadequate. Hundreds of educational institutions interchange students by the thousands while millions of men are being militarily prepared to interchange our bullets by the billions.

In all this, it is not our ideological discrepancies which cause conflict. It is our identities. All sides believe in physical coercion and violence. We all believe in continuing to put our intellectual resources into processes of power politics. All nations accept the principle of unrestricted nationalism. All seem to accept and base practice upon the erstwhile fact of human disunity and untrustworthiness.

E. THE RELIGIOUS FEATURE

The contribution of religious organizations to war is ideological and emotional. As in the case of other educational institutions, the chief contribution here is in what is done to the individual and, through him, to other institutions. Summarily speaking, religion contributes heavily to the moral components in the total pattern. Seldom is a church accused of unpatriotic behaviour. Though designed for integration of humanity, it seems forced (for political and economic reasons) to go along with the antagonistic drift of a culturally estranged and politically segregate race. By going along with the drift, the religious institutions contribute to it.

Whatever the claim to divine or supernatural origin and special favour, the religious organization is, after all, managed by men. As men, 'church' men are amenable to environmental pressure and inner limitations as truly as are men who manage other institutions. There is here no insulation or independence from other institutions. The individuals who compose the other types of organizations tend to be the same individuals who make up the religious groups. Interlocking boards of directors are only part of this painful fact. Like other types, so, too, religious types have their economic supports and strictures. They too come under the supervision and surveillance of political agencies which are partisan—not global.

Much of the influence upon the individual is in the more or less silent support of profound assumptions rather than in explicit utterance. Between the lines is found support for the modern religious tenet that a man's duty to a politically bounded part of humanity is higher than his duty to the whole. The fact that man pays taxes heavily to national governments and little or none to a world government goes unnoticed and unchallenged.

Love and hostility are advocated in the same sermon. 'Gott mit uns' is not restricted to one language. Separation of church and state is seldom argued where inter-nation rivalry is concerned. The modern god of modern man is too often and too much the god of the state. Thus far, individual or corporate efforts to change this have been weak and ineffective.

F. THE MASS COMMUNICATION INSTITUTIONS

Combination of the severest features of economics and education is found in our agencies of press and radio, film and television. In terms of amount of capital outlay and of numbers of persons reached, our institutions of one-way communication have reached dangerous size. In a world of conflict, propaganda is natural if not inevitable. Most observers point out that true propaganda tells the truth but not the whole truth. If it is to become successful, it must tell that part of the truth which promotes or props up 'our' cause. In doing this, our propaganda agencies in all camps are true to their commitment to co-operate to antagonize that which others co-operate to support. Their tragic effect is to increase confusion and misunderstanding. What chance has the tiny individual with his tiny intellect and small amount of time in a world of such giant organizations of communication? Daily, a tremendous army of actors and editors and reporters, of columnists and commentators prepare and rehearse the lines for a most possible dramatic climax of human extinction. They daily fan the already prevailing winds of opinion in a world made dangerous by the 'evil' intentions of governments of other countries. The formula seems to be, 'Let's build trust in our government and hostility to its opponents or possible opponents'. Telling good things about the other man's nation seems a luxury which the individual can rarely afford.

All these groups of educational organizations—the mass communicational, the scholastic and the religious—share a common fate. They are interlocked within the overall material and psychological frame of reference. The climate of opinion in which they operate and which they cause is also their master. The pattern of attitude which supports them is the one they must support. This is the attitude of intra-group, intra-nation loyalty, trust and cooperation along with inter-nation hostility, distrust, and antagonism. Because these educational institutions (instructional, inspirational, informational) are partisan, they tend to report and teach and emphasize the facts favourable to 'our' side and unfavourable to others. Because we are partisan individuals (not by nature but by education), we tend to believe and remember one-sided factual emphasis and even, to some extent, demand it.

It should be recognized that this is a sketchy discussion of the over-all pattern of our interlocking and interdependent social institutions. Whole classes of institutions have been left out. For example, nothing has been said about the family of which there are several hundred million separate units. There are hundreds of thousands of groups organized along lines of profession or occupation, sociability and recreation. These too exert their pressure in the ocean of human organization.

We wish to repeat that the shortcomings and the irrationalities of human organizational activity can only be adequately appreciated by observing all the units as a pattern and noting the net effect and futility of the total pattern. For instance, if one studies the operation of the Foreign Office of Great Britain from a narrow British point of view, he might well be impressed with the brilliant amount of intelligence displayed. The same would be true of the men in charge of the foreign affairs of the U.S.S.R., and likewise the Department of State of the U.S.A. But let the visitor from Mars consider the joint behaviour of these three organizations and he might well conclude that men are the most irrational of earth's creatures. From the point of view of a narrow or partisan goal, we may be giving to our social relations the best of which we are capable. From the point of view of net effect upon humans as a whole, our behaviour is tragically deficient if not stupid.

Reorganization Called For

So what? Misorganization recognized means reorganization demanded. If we are misorganized, obviously our need is to reorganize.

Reorganization does not mean disorganization. Organization is indispensable as well as inevitable. We have been talking about a real world of real people with real needs served by real institutions. The need is not for less service. The need is for better service. What our institutions are giving us is a confusing mixture of curse and blessing. Obviously we cannot afford to dispense with the blessing. Our social malady calls for constructive social surgery guided by realistic discrimination.

Total elimination of present organizational pattern is not what we need to look for. Nor is it possible to keep things as they are. Nor can we afford to let nature (especially human nature) take its unsupervised course. Blind change by blind nature or blind men will not do. Two needs then stand out. The first need is courage. All men tend to fear change. Change is sure to come sooner or later, for better or worse. Let us abolish our undifferentiated fear of change. The change we need to fear is change that is blind and uninvited—uncontrolled by enlightened human interest. Let us beware of change that is brought on by narrow self-interest and short-sighted group interest. Above all we are justified in our fear of change brought on by man in his ignorance. Sheer inspiration or blind courage is not enough. To drive doggedly ahead with increased energy in our present directions will not save us. To turn everything upside down may merely substitute another kind of chaos for the kind we have. Changes we must make. But they must be appropriate.

The second need is for adequate knowledge if we are to achieve a valid fearlessness for change. We need to use the utmost of our rational, fact-finding, and creative processes in order to plot the safe route to a new institutional pattern—a route we can travel with confidence and without eventual disappointment. All this must be done in time. Precious time is tragically passing while the pot and the kettle call each other black. Time and talent must be generously invested to find out what institutional changes are needed and how they may be brought about. The need is for knowledge which nobody now knows.

What kind of knowledge is required? Essential to social progress is not only new knowledge but new kinds of knowledge. The knowledge now in the encyclopaediae and other weighty tomes on our library shelves apparently is inadequate. World Almanac type statistics are not sufficient. Our problem is not purely one of economic and of physical technique. More of the kind of knowledge recently produced by technical engineers and physical scientists seems especially suited to hastening the day of racial suicide.

The new knowledge needed is social and psychological. If the human mind is to survive, it must conquer its ignorance of itself. More must be known about our minds and the emotions or feelings which condition their operation. This new knowledge must deal with attitudes and beliefs. Our moral and social assets and liabilities cannot be adequately assessed by guess. We have to know more about human fear and faith, trust and distrust, and of the facts and fictions to which these are due. The nature of this new knowledge is illustrated in Chapter 8, where we discuss the need for better understanding through better communication. Naturally, at this stage of intellectual progress, we cannot tell much about the new knowledge needed. But it seems reasonable now to say that the most obvious need is to know more clearly each other's intent and potential intent. For purposes of organization or teamplay, co-ordination of action is essential. In a democratically successful society, there is great need for *mutual knowledge*. Without it the individual actors cannot co-ordinate their motions. Obviously, our need is for harmony of behaviour, i.e., unitary or concerted action. Unitary action requires unitary knowledge. Only when 'a' and 'b' know where each intends to go and by what route, can they synchronize and harmonize their movements. How are we to get this necessary unitary knowledge? The social world is enormous. By what method is it possible for each to have enough foreknowledge of each other's individual behavioural tendency or attitude and potential attitude to make corporate behaviour successful? This is the challenge to human intelligence. It is a job for reclaimed intellect presently pursuing lesser ends and so often prostituted to partisan and antagonistic uses.

No one can, on the basis of present knowledge, present an accurate and concrete blueprint of the new pattern of organization. This is a task for the organized effort of thousands of highly intelligent and skilled men and women. If our criterion is correct, we shall have to delete somehow from present organization those features which bring about mutual antagonism. We shall have to improve many of our present institutions and institute new ones to fill the gaps in the present pattern. Organizations which represent a part of the human family will have to be re-orientated and non-partisanly operated so that they will constitute no liability or disadvantage to any other part of the human family. These will have to be supplemented by organizations representing the race as a whole. This can best be illustrated now qualitatively by some of the specialized agencies of the United Nations, such as F A O and W H O, which concern themselves with the food and health needs of men throughout the world. Obviously, we shall need to expand and extend such organizations many thousandfold. As they now stand they are no match for the menace of global hunger and disease. A third type of organization which is greatly needed might be called an organization to improve organizations. The nearest illustration of this which we have is the U N itself, although at the present both qualitatively and quantitatively highly inadequate. We introduce it here as a token of the future in that it has been the promoter or foster parent of such specialized agencies as those just referred to. We would like to make a separate division and specify a fourth type of organization to constitute the brains of organization. If we are to find the new knowledge required to guide us in reorganization, we must search for it. Organization to support and organize the searchers is indispensable. Here we have our best, though very meagre, illustration in U N E S C O. A very small segment of this very inadequate organization is devoted to developing the new knowledge to guide the new world towards greater solidarity—politically and culturally.

We are fully aware that these present-day organizational illustrations are not inspiring in terms of their present performance, but we would say of them three things: (1) they are the best we have; (2) where they have qualitatively failed, it is where they have been guided by men under great pressure of partisan outlook and loyalty; (3) we are not justified in judging them by their effects so long as financial and moral support given them is so very, very meagre. We suggest that these institutions even qualitatively speaking represent only a scratch on the surface of our enormous corporate possibilities—most of all is this true of U N E S C O, whose highest function is intellectual co-operation towards world-wide goodwill. In this sort of thing resides the greatest opportunity for strategic improvement toward a reorganized society. Theoretically at least, our destiny depends upon those institutional arrangements which determine the way men use their highest intelligence. Human brain power must be rechannelled in new directions if we are to gain the understanding necessary for survival. It is a vain pretence to sing, 'I ain't gonna study war no more' as long as we keep giving such extensive support to scientific weaponeering and ignore new and necessary arrangements for men to make a living by the study of peace and harmony. This, then, looked at sociologically, is why we need a science of peace. We need an enterprise to find out how to reorganize. Nothing less valid and accurate and nothing less rapid than science will do.

The depth of the prison of ignorance in which we are organizationally locked must not be underestimated. We must prepare ourselves to face and pay the ransom price. Obviously our predicament is real—our dilemmas are widespread and difficult. These we dare not ignore. Unless men find the way to greater harmony, mankind is doomed.

The specific analysis presented in this chapter may not eventually prove the best starting-point. If there are better approaches, let's have them. The mystery of social reorganization may be only one of several secrets which our nature now holds locked in store for us. In any event, the great unlocking key is human intelligence. It is also the creator of unlocking devices.

Of late, human reason seems to have fallen into disrepute. Its usefulness is denied in certain areas of human bewilderment. Science, the brilliant and attractive handmaiden of human progress, is losing her reputation for purity of service and ability to fetch the unmixed blessings of truth.

We believe that our present predicament is due to a profoundly serious error for which there is a remedy. This over-all error in the use of the scientific method we wish now to discuss in the next chapter.

4
SCIENCE IN MISORDER

THE picture of a vast and complex misorganization of a world of helpless individuals, drawn in the past chapter, need not leave us hopeless. Intelligence and individual sanity are still with us. Science, the greatest embodiment of co-operative human intelligence, is highly incomplete. Its potential contribution is far from exhausted. In this chapter, we wish to introduce this ray of hope.

For the most part, lovers of peace have tragically overlooked this most powerful and potential, though ambiguous, asset of mankind. This phenomenon of science is so new and dazzling as to have a frightening and blinding effect upon us as we observe and attempt to interpret the modern social scene. In this chapter we want to discuss the nature and extent of its dangers and liabilities, and to point out the enormous opportunities for its redirection. The reader will please keep constantly in mind this positive goal. Redirection does not mean total renunciation. However much we may in these pages seem to be denouncing our unhappy scientific developments, we are not renouncing science *per se*. We are insisting, not upon rejection, but upon reclamation, reconstruction and redirection of this most precious and most ill-managed resource for human progress. Adequate evaluation requires that we face squarely the negative aspects of this most potent factor in modern cultural evolution.

The 'all-powerful method of science' has been a very decisive factor in modern social evolution. The grave aspects of our social misorganization cited in the last chapter are inseparable from the miracles of modern physical science and engineering. It is the success of human intelligence in science that has made the nations so big and strong and brought them face to face. Science has caused the release of power now held by individual men and nations which justifies their enormous fear of one another. It is science-born machinery in our factories that has made possible the fearful centralization of industry. Our science-born mechanisms make possible our huge institutions of mass media and propaganda. It is man's scientific effectiveness that makes it possible to co-ordinate the effort of individuals to deliver vast cargoes of destruction and death to opposite sides of the world.

SCIENCE AFFECTS SOCIAL ORGANIZATION

It is through our social institutions that science functions with regard to war preparation, war causation, and war participation. Our political institutions levy the tax with which to buy the time of individual scientists. Our military institutions operate as specialized and enormously oversized agents of politics. These command the services of great numbers of our brightest individuals. Industry rearranges its production line to produce the gadgets to serve the drift towards greater and greater war. By virtue of their enormous financial power, they seem to have ample resources for commandeering the time and intelligence of the most talented of our population. Our educational institutions operate within the 'ivory tower' to indoctrinate and to train in those disciplines which make men ever more powerful and more dangerous to one another. Our mass media institutions for communication not only use the products of the scientific laboratory to prepare and support our belligerency, more and more intense, but they also use the scientific method to measure their effects upon the mind of man. It must be remembered that, more and more, psychological warfare is growing and that, more and more, psychological warfare is scientific warfare. The one type of institution previously mentioned which seems to make little use of the scientific method is that of religion. What would happen here, if the religious and the scientific mood were more congenial, is hard to predict.

An important feature is the negative effect of science upon our human sensitiveness. We refer to the increasing distance between the killer and the killed. The efforts of an illiterate factory hand in a civilian plant become highly related to the death of a soldier or civilian on the other side of the world months or years later. What is said about the man who fashions munitions can be said about the citizen who unwittingly pays his income-tax, or the instructor who teaches the elements of scientific method to future weapon inventors. Science enables men to assassinate each other anonymously—to exchange mutual extinction 'sight unseen'. By the intricate and complex processes by which we operate, we can proceed with great devotion and sacrifice and false sense of duty not only to country but to truth itself, and thus pursue with clear conscience the otherwise morally forbidden. By virtue of these great distances, we can lead ourselves into thinking beautiful that which, at close range, would be highly repulsive.

War Appropriates Science

War has appropriated the power of science at two levels. First, it has appropriated the products of scientific research—the inventions and mechanisms through which human intelligence has endowed us with such a profusion of power—physical power. Most of the areas of scientific research have produced instruments or methods which have been seized upon by men at war with each other. War has seized for defensive or antagonistic purposes instruments which could and should have been used only constructively.

However, we are well advanced into a second and more serious stage of the appropriations of science by war. This is the appropriation of the process of scientific research. Throughout the world in industries, in universities, and in institutions specifically set up for war preparation purposes, there are laboratories equipped for research on the instruments suitable for destruction and death. These laboratories command the services of large numbers of brilliant and devoted young scientists. These carefully selected and talented persons, by virtue of their institution's assignments, use the utmost of their intelligence to make discoveries and invent products whose primary utility, and in some instances exclusive utility, is for purposes of waging war.

Here no longer is the controlling motive that of pure science. Naturally, here, the criterion of a successful invention is the number of persons we can kill or threaten to kill with the instruments evolved. We say 'naturally' because this is the indisputable logic of the programme of personal security through national security through the instrumentality of modern war. If we are to avoid this hideous criterion of successful intellectual and scientific work, we must evolve a non-belligerent and probably a non-antagonistic alternative for the achievement of personal and social destiny.

This characteristic appropriation of the method of science to the cause of international warfare is not limited to any one nation or group of nations. As an illustration of how it works in one nation, we can refer to the huge expenditures being made in the U.S.A. in connection with the Atomic Energy Commission. It has been estimated that some $6,000,000,000 was spent on research and technical development by this commission previous to 1952. As of June 1952, the estimated expenditures for each of the years 1952 and 1953 was over $1,700,000,000. How could the American Congress be motivated to appropriate such huge sums for a scientific project? The answer is that this is primarily an appropriation for war purposes. No peacetime or peace purpose research appropriation of this size has been known in the history of any nation. In contrast, the appropriation by this same national congress to support the National Research Foundation is $3,500,000, only a part of which rests on non-military motivation. In terms of international conflict, what happens in one nation almost inevitably happens in the others.

Nowhere is science so dangerous as when hitched to the partisan motive and nowhere is the partisan motive so vicious as when aided and abetted by the scientific method. On the other hand, nowhere will a limited amount of altruism go so far as when guiding science.

Through our misorganized social institutions we use the products and the methods of science with ever increasing danger and chances of devastation. In science, human ingenuity has reached its highest levels of constructive creativeness. However, in effect the trend seems more and more to be construction for destruction and creation for extinction.

The two-way contradictory effects of science make its appraisal difficult. It functions both to help and to hinder progress in human satisfaction. Vast contributions have been made in lifesaving devices, including disease immunization and other hygienic processes. There are thousands of hospitals and laboratories where, through science, millions of men share their blood with the victims of accident and disease. On the other hand, science has increased immensely the possible profusion of bloodshed on the field of battle. Science has made possible threat of bacteriological and atomic warfare.

An over-all perspective of science is needed, a careful scrutiny of scientific objectives is required. The fallacy dies hard that science is an unmitigated blessing and that scientific devotion to truth can only bless and never curse mankind—regardless of the truth sought. The first atomic blast at Almagordo did much to blast this notion. Behold more and more willingness to criticise science and scientists and science supporters: let us take care that this criticism be eventually constructive, else there can be no hope.

Proper Science in Improper Order

In 1943 Raymond Fosdick asked, 'Is it after all possible that Science has given us the right answers in the wrong order?' An affirmative answer to this question becomes daily more obvious. This concept can go a long way to explain the appalling and disappointing miscarriage of the scientific hope of previous decades. The faulty outcome of human intellectual activity is a function of the faulty directions which it has taken. The fault is not so much in what science has done but in what science has not done.

Two broad observations are now clear. Very unsatisfactory is the progress man has made in social harmony. Amazing is the progress made in physical power. In terms of real outcome, mankind in its scientific capacity seems to have sought first not the kingdom of social harmony, but the kingdom of physical power. By virtue of our scientific knowledge, we are now able to melt mountains and to bridge oceans. We know tragically little how to dissolve human conflicts and structure an adequately broad base for human co-operation. We have sought out the mysteries of atoms. We have ignored or trifled with the mystery of attitudes. The crying need now seems not for material or nuclear fission, but for social or political fusion.

To spell out this appalling discrepancy in human progress, we ask the reader to bear with us while we discuss seven big interrelated facts: (1) the fact of social conflict; (2) the fact of human purpose; (3) the fact of social harmony; (4) the fact of human physical power; (5) the fact of physical power increase; (6) the fact of social harmony deficiency; and (7) the fact of the role of science in present-day discrepancy between physical and social progress. To keep the total picture more clearly in mind we will allow considerable overlap in the presentation of these seven facts.

All told they add up to what appears as the most dangerous error thus far committed by the human species.

The Fact of Conflict

No one can look broadly at present-day human relations without being impressed with the widespread fact of conflict. In some form or other, it goes on wherever persons or groups are in contact. It extends back in the history of the race as far as we can see. In our moods of psychological depression, there *seems* to be no end as we look into the future. It ranks exceedingly high among the causes of human tragedy. It pays enormous negative dividends in terms of poverty, disease, war, and almost every aspect of human misery. It defeats our profoundest ideals. The greatest argument against democracy is 'See how they quarrel among themselves when they have no over-lord'.

It is an aspect of human society which seems to defy our bravest and most skilful efforts. We make changes. We rearrange our procedures. We eliminate conflict here only to see it pop up yonder. We learn new ways to do new things, but not without conflict. We learn to put nations together, but not together harmoniously. In certain areas of the planet we succeed in raising the standard of living but not the social standard of living together.

Philosophers have long concerned themselves with the concept of *evil*. We recommend, instead, the concept of conflict. Instead of asking, 'Why is there so much evil in the world', let us ask, 'Why are men everywhere so much in conflict?' The change of word does not change our condition, but it should make a solution more hopeful. It should bring us closer to an operational point of view. Conflict is not quite so difficult to tag. It is more capable of objective recognition. It is clearly a function of people. It is a perceptible attribute of observable human behaviour. Though it contains many hidden aspects, its presence is obvious in the overt behaviour of real people in real situations.

This is not to say that we adequately understand it. Far from it. The mystery of conflict is the argument for a science of human relations. The why or how of conflict is one way to state the central target not only of a science for peace, but of social science in general. It is a target to be successfully aimed at, not primarily by our emotions, but by our intellect. It is, in part, a subjective matter requiring an unaccustomed amount of objective study.

To summarize, we are, sociologically speaking, creatures of conflict. This is due to our social psychology. Psychologically speaking, what are we?

Conflict and Purpose

We are socially creatures of conflict because psychologically and individually we are creatures of purpose. If we understand too poorly the sociology of conflict, it is because we understand so inadequately the psychology of purpose. In this realm, our questions are likely to be crude and unsustained. Our answers are likely to be too quick and short and abortive. When men are asked to explain what lies back of this worldwide, timewide factor of conflict, the trite tendency is to attribute it to human nature. Mark Twain referred to it as 'this damned human nature'. For constructive ends, we would delete the damnation and call it *purposeful* human nature. Conflict flows from the purposeful nature of man. Man, to be man, has to live by his purposes. By its very nature, human purpose works towards fulfilment. At any moment, the purposive individual is seen to be engaged in facilitating those processes which lead to a desired end. This facilitation means pushing things around. To achieve his ends, each individual has to arrange objects and bring about events in his environment. This environment includes other persons. These other persons also have purposes, ends, goals, which they pursue. One of the most essential characteristics of this thing we call purpose is its autonomous or independent nature. This means that purposes are not born harmonious with one another; hence the natural and widespread fact in human social life is everywhere apparent that purposes collide with and run contrary to each other. To the extent that this is true within one individual, we call it lack of integration. To the extent that this contradiction takes place among persons of a given society, we say we lack social harmony or social integration. The purposes of one's contemporaries can constitute obstacles to one's purpose fulfilment. A common and not unnatural impulse is that these obstacles—that is, the other person's purposes—require modification or removal. To make a long story short, purpose-fulfilment of one individual becomes purpose-frustration for someone else. This frustration has many degrees of virulence. It often leads to the purpose to eliminate or exterminate the frustrator. Thus it comes about that a man's greatest problem or greatest hazard often is other purposeful men.

By this time some of our readers have brought up an old and semi-comforting thought and are asking, 'But, isn't some conflict desirable?' Our reply is at two levels. If conflict is a blessing, why is it so rare to find any great and accepted moral and social philosopher who advocates it? Why do we not make an effort to cultivate it in any of our serious associations among human adults? Primarily the places where men deliberately attempt to initiate or promote conflict are in those social situations where they wish to weaken or destroy an opposing social organization.

In the second place, let us recognize that there are levels of conflict which are more disastrous than others. Then let us agree on our recognition that unless our present trend is diverted, mankind will likely reach a level of disaster-prone conflict suited to end our civilization or possibly terminate our race. Whatever need we may have for conflict of one sort or another now or at some distant future time, we cannot long survive with the kind and amount now going on. Surely no one would object to our finding out how to effect a reduction in the degree and intensity of present-day human antagonism and hostility.

The Fact of Harmony

Let us now make explicit an assumption doubtless held by all that conflict is a matter of degree. Our concept of conflict refers not to an absolute. Men or their purposes are never 100 per cent in conflict. As surely as there is a degree of conflict in human society, there is a degree of harmony. The widespread tendency of autonomous purposes, of more or less independent purposers, to clash, is only a part of our universal observation. It is just as inevitable, since man is the kind of sympathetic social creature that he is, that purposes will fail to collide or clash. Harmony is at least as inevitable as conflict. By conscious communality of purpose, men co-operate throughout time and space. At somewhat lower levels, conflict is reduced by various restraints either externally or internally imposed. Without a great amount of co-operation and co-ordination our modern civilization would have been impossible.

In any sizeable social unit, both harmony and conflict exist side by side. This seems to be the unbroken rule to date. However, the ratio between the two varies. Let us call this the H:C ratio variable. Not merely the amounts of each, but the relative amounts of each vary from place to place, from time to time, from relation to relation. There are times when each of us acts upon the assumption that he can do something about this ratio—about increasing harmony and decreasing conflict. This means that he assumes that this variable is to some extent under his control. Nor is this merely a short-lived and idle assumption. Men perennially yearn not only for victory over defeated adversaries, but for the elimination of conflict and of the necessity for adversaries and defeat. But the ideal and the goal so often and so much elude us. Most of us would assume that our actual control is far below our potential control of this H:C ratio. This control represents the greatest single factor in human control over human destiny. High now in our destiny is the question of international peace. The ideal of peace is the ideal of increasing our harmony at the international level. However, the ugly fact remains. Conflict among men and groups exists. Harmony among human purposes continues at a level far too low for comfort and for safety.

But what's new about this? Human culture and even the species itself seems to have originated and developed in the midst of struggle and conflict and in spite of greatly limited harmony. Men have always been dangerous to one another (as well as helpful to one another). Hence we need to turn our attention next to the fact of power and of power increase.

Purpose and Power

Purpose and purpose contradiction is only one aspect of human behaviour. The fact of physical power is as inescapable in social science as is the fact of human purpose. In actual life, power and purpose are universal and inseparable. Power makes purpose possible and meaningful. Only as there is prospect of enough power to carry out a given purpose can that purpose develop.

The kind of power we are talking about may be defined as the ability of persons to manipulate physical matter in the interest of human purpose. It would be more simple and very inspiring if we could stop here and say that power only functions to satisfy human want and fulfil human purpose. But we must repeat that as long as men's purposes conflict, the ability of purpose facilitation carries with it the possibility of purpose frustration. In actuality, then, we are forced to define power as ability held by a person enabling him to facilitate *or* frustrate the purpose of one or more persons. Gross power can be measured by our ability not only to get what we want but to prevent others from getting what they want. Power turns out to be not only power by men over matter, but power by men over men.

The danger from conflict is proportionate to men's power. Our alarm is justified as we view our ancient tendency toward discord alongside of modern power. Violent conflict between two small boys on the playground does not alarm an observer as does that of two grown men whose fists have become harder and arms stronger. Moreover, if these two adults hold their fingers on triggers of loaded revolvers, the alarm of the observer becomes much greater. What happens to small boys as they grow older has happened to adults as civilization has grown older. The race and its civilization could once tolerate discord unlimited. In the presence of power, more and more unlimited, such discord is more and more fatal.

Power Intensified

One of the most striking observations to be made in all human history is the recent tremendous increase in human power. In certain industrialized portions of the world, this observation is so common that we are likely to overlook its significance. Compared to his primitive ancestor, modern industrial individual man has the equivalent of several hundred human slaves. Science-born mechanisms have, in effect, changed enormously the physical dimensions of the individual. Inanimate nature drives our machinery at the touch of a button. It propels our boats, our cars, our trains, our planes. It produces and preserves our foods. It fabricates our clothing and our shelter to ever higher levels of durability and comfort and convenience.

There is a great ambiguity, however, in the present spectacle of human advancement. Intelligent people disagree sharply as to the reality of our progress. Are we glad or sad at what we see? This depends on whether one views, on the one hand, merely the increase in human power, or, on the other hand, the use of power; whether one assumes merely the constructive use of power or whether one is sensitive to the destructive uses. We *may* note the vast increase in man's power dimension without noting its unhappy uses.

We are aware of vast increase in the stride of our legs figuratively speaking and in the range of our voices. In transportation and communication, our progress is almost unbelievable. But how does this affect the social quality of our actual behaviour? In contrast to the travel drudgery of centuries, we now glide along the countryside at 60 or 80 miles per hour with the greatest of ease and comfort. At much higher speeds, we transcend mountains and cross oceans. But for what purpose? It may be that of a man with a happy family on a vacation trip crossing a continent. Or it may be that of a man leading a blitzkrieg across a national boundary to demolish houses, separate families, and slaughter innocent children and helpless adults. The wings by which we fly may carry us on educational or economic missions of good will and co-operation or they may not. They may carry the cargo of the greatest potential destruction to life which the age of radiation has developed.

As with the uses we make of our new legs, so it is with the uses we make of our new voices. Man's voice has increased in range to match the dimensions of our globe. But what are the air waves saying? The contents of our message may be broadly and openly distributed to serve the purposes of mutual aid and co-operation. Or they may not. They may be transmitted guardedly and with great secrecy, generating hostility and serving the ends of frustration and antagonism.

Power over matter includes power over man. We have said that we are here discussing human physical power, and that this in turn means the power of a human person over matter. It may be argued by some that man is spiritual as well as physical. However spiritual he may be, man as we know him and understand him must exert his impulses—must facilitate his purposes, spiritual or otherwise, in part at least, by what he does to the materials in his environment. Any human power, therefore, is not only a power by man, but potentially at least, a power over man. It has been said that science has literally given man the power to move mountains. In the sense in which this is true, it is also true that men have been given the power to move mountains on to or on top of other men. A mountain of violence was released on several thousand human beings in the city of Hiroshima, August 5, 1945. Thus far human ingenuity seems to have been unable to make a great extension of our power without extending this power over one another.

The anticipation of the negative use of power is an essential factor in human conflict. The mechanisms of conflict, involving as they do the elements of fear, suspicion, and retaliation, are greatly aggravated by our great increase in power. Previously we indicated that conflict between the purposes of two individuals brings on the desire to frustrate and to counter-frustrate and, in many instances, to eliminate one another. At these more virulent levels, it is only natural that great fear should arise through the anticipation of frustration and elimination. It is the natural behaviour of a rational, alert, imaginative being not only to retaliate when force is used upon him negatively or destructively, but to anticipate such frustration or destruction and to retaliate in time to avoid personal disaster. All our moralizing thus far has not succeeded in abolishing this widespread characteristic in human behaviour.

The modern interaction between consciousness of increasing danger from increasing power and belief in the necessity of ever increasing power to minimize our danger is an instance of man being trapped by his culture. This terrible toll upon human trust and human hope seems destined to continue as long as power increases and conflict continues. The effort of the nations to achieve security through greater power to retaliate becomes increasingly a tragic mockery. The notion that the best defence is offence plays an important role in war and war preparation. Preparation for defence and preparation for aggression are too hard to distinguish. The modern paraphernalia of death 'essential' to one are largely identical with those which are essential to the other.

Power politics was never a morally satisfying technique. But in the past, its inaccuracies, its errors, its accidents were such as to permit the race to survive. Power increase changes, but does not improve, power politics. Formerly the bargaining quality was the number of mobile regiments of infantry with rifles. Now it is more and more the size and mobility of the nuclear stockpile.

Shortly after the announcement of the atomic bomb, one

atomic scientist said that it was to be hoped that the dangerousness of the new weapons would cause mankind to abolish war. This hope is not dead but sadly deferred. What has happened? We may have increased our *wish* for peace but not our *will*—not our peace investment. Instead we invest increasingly in armament 'improvement'. In both quantity and quality, our weapons change enormously. But is this progress? From the point of view of the safety of either individuals or nations, this is not progression but retrogression. As our power becomes greater, it tends to become more unmanageable. As another atomic scientist has said, 'The atomic bomb is not a precision instrument. It is as likely to kill a Democrat as a Republican'. Prime ministers and common soldiers are equally unsuited to atomic heat. A century ago the range of a rifle or of a cannon was a matter of a few hundred yards. Today, jet planes and guided missiles are designed to seek their targets hundreds and even thousands of miles away. Early rumours regarding the hydrogen bomb referred to the problem of toning it down so that it would wipe out only one nation at a time. What next? How long can this kind of 'progress' continue? Surely the hydrogen bomb is not the end of the genealogy of weapons, unless man or war becomes quickly eradicated.

As long as the problem of conflict remains unsolved, the hope for progress through more power is false. Purposeful men require power, but men in conflict can stand only so much. Purpose without power is futility, but too much power with too little harmony spells calamity. Ordinary penchant for conflict with extraordinary power brings extraordinary peril.

Harmony Lacking

In the midst of ever increasing power, man appears ever more helpless. Our power increase is real—our progress appears false. Why? Something must be lacking. Daily it becomes more foolish to judge a civilization by its gross display of power—ignoring the amount of conflict, cruelty and misery. The true measure can only be made in relation to human purpose, human desire and human satisfaction. When one man's power is pitted against another man's power, power cancels out. When one man's achievement has to be accompanied by another man's frustration, the net satisfaction to mankind as a whole diminishes toward zero.

The true goal of civilization is to increase not merely the sum total of power, but the amount used effectively. Atomic power can be no asset to human betterment unless effectively controlled to this end. Atomic energy discovery is not true progress unless and until the nations harmonize. What is true of atomic energy is true of numerous and, perhaps, far greater power discoveries yet possible. Whatever may be true in the distant future, the need now is to reduce our conflict.

That men are capable of deliberately increasing their harmony has been demonstrated in a great many instances. But the bright and dark elements of the picture are badly mixed. Recently the dark pigments seem to have been gaining over the bright. Progress, however, is best thought of as neither impossible nor inevitable. Our progress in human harmonization or unification has been very pronounced, but irregular and alarmingly incomplete. Note the progression in the past several thousand years in the growth and size of the political unit. Families have been combined into tribes, tribes into cities or sections, cities or sections into nations, smaller nations into larger ones. A certain amount of violence-immunity has thus been vouchsafed within political groups of ever increasing populational and geographic scope. This has its promising side and should give us reason for great expectation. As political aggregations grow greater, however, so does the size of our wars. The goal of history would seem to be, and this stands out with gleaming possibility for many of us, the all-inclusive aggregation of the human family into one unit of sufficient political and psychological solidarity to eliminate the fear that man will exterminate himself by war. On the tragic side is the great extent to which these mergers take place in connection with conquest and not with free and deliberate co-operation.

But we are far short of this goal of one world politically. Thus far we are politically inept and in arrears. We have failed to separate governments and war. We are proud of two legacies from the past—that of law and that of brotherhood. But we have not discovered how to operate law without coercion and the threat of force. We continue to associate government with violence. The relation between the state and the individual remains confused and unsolved. War has been referred to as politics at the level of bloodshed. War we couldn't have without government. Can we achieve warless government? This is our challenge. It is a challenge to any human who thinks enough of his race to want it to continue. Even within each national unit often our democratic progress threatens to become a tragic mockery. Tyranny or the threat of tyranny is always near. Science has made terrifyingly possible powerful implementation to those who would 'tyrannize over the minds of men'. Oppression of minorities is never totally absent from any continent. These unholy combinations of unity and dissension, of love and hate, give the thoughtful observer great caution in assuming that there has been much net progress in the matter of harmonizing human relations. Doubtless many elements of harmony are inherent in our individual nature and in our culture. But ours is still a society of conflict of disturbing proportions.

Let us be explicit about the relativity in our present situation. Neither great power nor low harmony is necessarily fatal, except in proportion to each other. An increase in physical power would have been no hazard to human society had it been accompanied or preceded by an adequate increase in harmony. But this has not happened. Not yet.

We have had similar notations about the social scene which may confuse us if we are not careful. For instance, there is a common and ambiguous phrase: 'the social lag'. Sometimes this refers to the lag of social progress behind physical progress or social science behind physical science. Sometimes it is referred to as the lag of practice behind theory, or sometimes as the lag of art or religion or education behind science. At risk of being charged with over-simplification we urge careful consideration of the simple concept of *too much power with too little harmony*. Reverse it if you wish and say too little harmony with too much power. We emphasize that it is relative. The discrepancy between these two lines of progress increases daily, and daily becomes increasingly ominous. We will hereafter refer to this as the unfortunate power-harmony ratio, P:H, or as the power-harmony imbalance. This simple concept must be kept clear if we are to think realistically about its cause and cure. This concept rests on the assumption that, for a given amount of power, there is a minimal amount of harmony necessary for human progress to continue (at least cultural and maybe biological). This evolution is now dangerously threatened by the present and increasing power-harmony imbalance. Now for the cause of this imbalance.

The Cause of Our Plight

Let us divide the question into two parts. First, how has power come to increase so much? Secondly, how has harmony come to improve so little? Let us take up first the cause of physical power increase.

All considerations point unmistakably to the factor of physical science. Whatever the cause or effect of modern scientific activity, it seems inescapable that here we have a vital link. Without this connecting link there could not have developed the chain of events which has led from weakness of primitive life to the modern might of our atomic age. There are certain facts about the way things happen (or can be made to happen) in the physical universe which have recently become known, which enable man better to carry out his material wishes. In every instance of power advance, we can note this factor of increased knowledge.

The evidences of this are all about us. Whence our power to fly? The human body has grown no flying wings unto itself. But the human mind has (by science) added unto itself flying knowledge. For a thousand centuries, however much man envied the birds, he was unable to fly enough to skip over one fair-sized treetop. At the beginning of the scientific era, to encircle the globe required more in months than is now required in days. Only two or three centuries ago, we were ignorant of the circulation of the blood and universally unaware of a germ or a hormone. Science-born knowledge now enables us to expect to live twice as long as then. Speeches and symphonies which originate in London are now heard in Lima, Seattle, Warsaw, Nangapur, Nairobi, Sydney. The tiny human ear has been stretched to cover six continents. To whom are we indebted for this? Faraday, Maxwell, Marconi, and thousands of other men dedicated to the scientific search for new knowledge.

The indispensable tool, not only for manipulating our complex modern technology, but for discovering and initiating it, is human intelligence. This is an old instrument shifted into a new key. It has become a tool-inventing tool. How this new use developed in the way and in the direction which it did is still much of an unsolved mystery. Since science has so vitally affected human history, and since it threatens in the immediate future to affect progress much more, and with such great uncertainty for good or ill, the problem of its adequate guidance should be given a high order of priority on the immediate agenda of social science and social technology. Now let us emphasize two aspects about mankind's affair with science—its human causation and it inadvertence.

Science is a human social affair. Whatever has happened has happened by human participation—human effort under the mandate of millions of separate human decisions. By thousands of financial and vocational choices, enormous resources of manpower and money-power are commandeered towards the altar of ever greater knowledge. Thus by many interacting decisions, men have become equipped, organized and disposed for behaviour in a vast, interlocking intellectual enterprise of research and education. This enterprise continues to feed into the scientific and technological processes whereby ever greater increments of power are added with ever greater speed. Truly, man has only begun to open up the floodgates of new knowledge for new power. Will he need to exterminate himself at this very early stage? Could this become the irony of ironies? Could this phase of extreme dedication to truth prove to be a fatal dedication to death?

And yet science in its totality, is, to a marked degree, an inadvertent outcome. It has arisen and developed without anyone's adequate foresight, without any over-all plan or design. No single individual or group of individuals has deliberately and consciously guided its long-time course of development. It was stated in Chapter 1 that no single individual or group of individuals can be identified as planning the end of our race or our civilization. As our culture has had no over-all design or guidance, and as our pattern of social organization has developed without being adequately guided by the ideal of over-all world unity, so it is with our science. No philosopher, no statesman, no scientist has designed or planned the course which physical science has taken. Science has been propagated and nurtured by the greatest of intellects. This most powerful giant has operated without the benefit of an oversoul or mind to question it and to guide it humanistically. Hence no one need be astonished at its great human uncertainty—its social ambiguity.

Let us turn to the second part of our inquiry into the cause of our alarming power-harmony imbalance. Why has social harmony shown such relatively slow and uncertain and inadequate improvement? This time our answer is the absence of science;

science by default. Harmony in human relations has not increased comparably because it has had to go on without the full blessing of an all-powerful science. Science did increase physical power but science did not increase social harmony. If this highly simplified statement can become acceptable, then we are ready for the further statement that *power-harmony imbalance has been brought about by science in misorder.*

Back of this last statement, there is an important assumption which it is the purpose of this book to elucidate and support. This is the assumption that science could have done and yet may do as much for our harmony as it has done for our power. Unawareness of and lack of faith in this assumption is itself responsible for the enormous error of achieving the increase of physical power instead of and before achieving sufficient increase of social harmony. The author's purpose in this book is to help to achieve rapidly this awareness and faith.

The scientific error is one of relativity of timing of the two lines of development. The proper time for greater power is after and not before greater harmony. Harmony has been, and increasingly is, our more urgent need. Except for bad timing, there is nothing wrong about any increase in human physical potency. Our misfortune is that this increase has been achieved before solving the problem of human social unity.

Recently there has been quite an increase of scientific research into human relations at the partisan level. Economists, psychologists, sociologists, anthropologists, and philosophers are now being increasingly employed by partisan groups or nations for purposes of intra-group or national unity. To a very definite degree, then, this is a continuation of previously mentioned practice of co-operation for antagonism. It is still too early to know fully the outcome of this new and rapidly rising development in social research, but it is now not too soon to realize that unguided or partisanly motivated social science is not the answer to our yearning for human unity.

The Remedy

What is the cure? The cure for science out of order is science reordered. The cure for wrong investment of our intellectual energies is reinvestment. Let us watch our tense. It is not merely true that we *have* misordered science—that we *have* misdirected our intelligence. We *are*, through misorganization, misusing scientific method. We *are* misdirecting our intelligence. The source of new knowledge for improved harmony (as of power increase) up to now and in the foreseeable future is human intelligence. Men are daily operating at high levels of intelligence and organization to get more of what we already have too much of. This spells tragedy for humans by human intelligence. It might well be called *the* intellectual tragedy. This tragedy is not to be averted by renouncing intelligence—by turning our back on the scientific method *per se*. The situation calls for scientific or intellectual redirection.

Not only is there a great dearth of scientific laboratories for highly expert research in the problem of harmonious human relations, but the machinery of organized and formal education does little to prepare the talent or make ready the attitude for such 'Laboratories'. The reciprocal relation between the classroom and the laboratory is important. Educational communication and scientific creation of knowledge must seek an optimal pattern of reciprocity. But whatever the relative roles of distributive and creative intelligence may be, *a shift of intellectual commitments and channellings is called for*.

As stated in the preceding chapter, social evolution must be given a new direction. There must be welded a new chain of causes and consequences. The crucial link in this chain is scientific *search* for a harmony know-how. Antecedent to this step there will need to be preparations or background developments, including the preparation of scientists with new skills or technologies, but most of all, with new orientation. As scientific knowledge is produced, the development of expert technicians may be required for its application. The important thing to remember is that the research is crucial. Without the process for developing the scientific knowledge, all other work remains impossible—all other effort futile.

RECAPITULATION

If human institutions are misorganized, let's reorganize our institutions. If we don't know how, let's use our intelligence to find out how. The first order is to organize or reorganize for better direction of our intelligence. As indicated in Chapter 2, this does not mean disorganization, because co-operation is essential to corporate society and organization is essential to co-operation. Moreover, it cannot be done by organization for co-operation for antagonism. It is essential that our organizing be guided by nonpartisan motivation. As we will indicate in Chapter 11, this reorganization will have to be done by concerned individuals who associate and pool their economic, intellectual, and moral resources.

If we have organized our intelligence in the wrong direction, let's make a shift. If our power-harmony ratio is unbalanced, let's use all our resources to balance it up. If this requires new knowledge, let's search for it. If a search for new knowledge requires a new science, let's develop it. If the time is short, let us do it with great speed. As Karl Menninger has said, 'In science man found a slave. With the world set on fire, it is time we reordered our slave'. What is holding us back?

5
IDEOLOGICAL BLOCKADES TO A SCIENCE OF PEACE

WHEN theory and practice contradict, there must be a cause. In contrast to this imperative need for a pronounced and speedy shift of our intellectual energy, is the appalling fact that at this moment in history there is perceptibly no such shifting. Apparently we are not reordering science. Why? What in the mind of man is preventing a scientific attack upon the number one problem of how the institution of war can be eliminated from human culture? In this chapter we wish to discuss certain objections which are frequently raised against our hope for a science of harmony and integration.

PEACE KNOW-HOW IS LACKING

First we wish to take time to discuss one basic assumption on which this chapter and this book are based. This we hope was made explicit in the past three chapters. It is, however, so basic to this chapter that we want to deal with it again explicitly at this point. The assumption is this: *the knowledge necessary for effective peace action is not now possessed by man.* The necessary facts are not known by any one person or identifiable group of persons. Simply stated, *Peace Know-how is lacking.*[1]

The greatest evidence for our peace know-how lack is the fact of war—the continuing fact of war. We realize that there can be other explanations of why war continues. There are other factors operating in causing men to continue to support this horrifying institution. But ignorance is surely one.

The force of this consideration increases greatly as we include in the concept of war the fact of war preparation. Not only periodic wars but continuous preparation as policy and practice of all major nations continues. It continues at continuously higher

[1] If the reader is strongly inclined to accept this assumption as a fact he may wish to skip the next few pages in which we present some very general considerations in its support.

levels of virulence and violence. Each passing day makes it more clear that this institution is the greatest evil to afflict mankind—an evil inconsistent with human survival. The necessity for peace grows ever more inescapable. And yet war continues.

Not only is the fact of war and war preparation a past and present fact; it seems to be a future fact. Our past record and present efforts *are* martial. Our future intentions *are* martial. We train and invent. We appropriate and build. We make gigantic plans not for war's cessation, but for the wars of tomorrow. Why? One answer is that we are trapped. We don't know how to get out of it.

One of the greatest evidences of our confused helplessness is in the extent to which people are willing to subscribe to such a highly illogical formula as peace through war or war preparation. The illogicality of this has become apparent from the record surrounding World Wars I and II. We pour out our money and devote the ultimate of our manhood to the proposition that war preparation is a step toward peace. When and where are the other steps? Our lack of know-how for peace can account for the fact of relative silence and inaction regarding any other steps. For instance, one of our more advanced nations, France, spent in 1951 more than one thousand times as much on its colonial war in Asia as it spent on its proportionate share of support of U N E S C O, which is seated in this same country and which is dedicated (on a very tiny budget) to war's termination. Other national governments, larger and smaller, appropriate 10 to 60 per cent of their budgets to their departments of military defence. Practically no nation spends as much as one per cent on U N and its specialized agencies combined. None of the nations has a Department of Peace, and apparently none is contemplated. If one suggests to an expert in political science that a nation which operates a fifty-billion-dollar Defence Department should have at least a billion-dollar Peace Department, he is likely to be met with the question, 'Well, what could a Peace Department do?' Nowhere do we see any effort *to prevent war* which is at all quantitatively comparable to the effort to prepare *to wage war*. Such minor efforts as we see at war prevention are primarily for war postponement. In a word, our bona fide peace effort is exceedingly low. This lack of peace effort strongly suggests a lack of peace know-how.

Note the astounding contrast between our negligible anti-war activity and various non-war activities. There are tens of millions of us engaged in each of scores of so-called peaceful pursuits. There are armies of workers for transportation, for communication, for agriculture, for clothing, for health, for education. We have trouble explaining why no army of workers to prevent war —the greatest interruption to all these activities. Why the oversight? Millions of men are kept continuously at work building more or less fireproof buildings and none at eliminating the hazard of atomic heat. Why all this activity to talk ourselves into contributing and collecting human blood, and such great inaction (such apparent indifference) toward eliminating the enterprise which so long has spilled human blood over plains and hillsides and diluted it with the waters of all the oceans?

Why this widespread inertia toward this ever mounting threat to both our security and our freedom and all else we value? This, of course, is an appalling mystery not to be lightly disposed of. No single sentence of explanation can be adequate. But we know of none that goes further and is more pregnant of practical realism than this simple suggestion that though there are men everywhere who care, they do not seem to know what to do about it.

We have used the term 'inertia'. We prefer it to 'indifference'. We suggest that a distinction be made between the desire for peace and the will for peace. We suggest that this is essentially the difference between abstract belief in peace and concrete effort for peace. This difference, in turn, goes along with difference between concern merely over the goal of world peace in contrast to a concern with the means as well. But unless something is known of the practical means of achieving the goal, it is difficult if not impossible to express practically our concern. How better can one account for the widespread *apparent* indifference of hundreds of millions of people threatened with obliteration by atomic warfare? How better to diagnose this phenomenon of inaction than a social and moral paralysis born of a sense of helplessness coupled with a natural desire to put out of one's mind a fear for which one has no other and no real cure? Why face that part of reality which one cannot negotiate? Only when given a realistic remedy within their reach, can men be expected to act. Zest for any enterprise or goal, however essential and otherwise meaningful, is impossible without some hopeful vision or practical pattern of action.

IDEOLOGICAL BLOCKADES TO A SCIENCE OF PEACE 59

The continuing lack of peace and the widespread lack of peace effort might be thought of as indirect evidence that peace know-how is lacking. Let us turn now to three types of more direct consideration. What do common men say about their peace knowledge when they are asked pointedly? What do our social and political and educational leaders say and what are they silent about when they come face to face with the enigma of human conflict at the level of international war? What do our knowledge-distributing institutions of education purport to have on tap pertinent to real ends of real peace?

In a nation-wide survey in the U.S.A. in 1946, the National Opinion Research Centre asked a representative sample of persons: 'Can you think of anything that you personally can do that would help prevent another war?' Sixty-four per cent said 'NO'. When the remaining 36 per cent were asked to specify, they gave responses which were quite general and not convincingly relevant and realistic, such as—'use my right to vote', 'practise Christianity', 'pray', 'teach peace', 'become informed', 'live right', 'stop talking and thinking war', 'stop propaganda', 'mind my own business'. (To quote from the survey report)—'That people do not have a clear idea of what they can actually *do* to implement their desire for peace, however, is suggested by the generality of the answers of many of the 36 per cent who do make suggestions. And it is significant that even these answers often echo the feeling that individual effort means little.'

When conducting informal surveys on this point, it becomes evident that the common citizen assumes that others have the know-how for peace even though he does not. As one adult newspaper vendor put it to the writer, 'Gee, I hadn't thought about it. If the guys up at the top don't know, who am I to think about it?' In this age of high organization, has not one a right to assume the existence somewhere of adequate expertness for this as for other jobs? What do our political and other leaders know in this connection? It is probably scarcely necessary to do much more than remind the reader that when high political and educational leaders emphasize the need of putting an end to war, there is very seldom anything definitely said about the means. In a speech at Boston in 1951, General MacArthur said, 'This experience (in Korea) again emphasizes the utter futility of modern war—its complete failure as an arbiter of international dissensions. Its threat must be abolished if the world is to go on; and if it does not go on, it will go under . . . each war becomes increasingly savage as the means for mass killing are further developed. You cannot control war; you can only abolish it.' He indicates the need for 'enterprise, vision, and courage to try a new approach', but does not say what the new approach is.

At the time when Bernard Baruch presented the U.S. Atomic Energy Control Plan to the U N Atomic Energy Commission, he said, 'we are here confronted with a problem not of science but of ethics.' Mr. Baruch did not indicate how we are to get at this problem of ethics. We seriously submit the proposition that this absence of a suggestion indicates an absence of knowledge of appropriate procedure. Surely, if a leader of Mr. Baruch's proportions had known how to achieve harmony among nations on the subject of atomic energy, he would not have withheld this information.

At about the same time of Mr. Baruch's report, Arthur Compton, Chancellor of Washington University, said, 'Mankind will have to grow in moral stature before it can safely play with atomic fire'. Nothing is said about how this growth is to take place. Is there any evidence that it is taking place? And if so, rapidly enough to win 'the race between education and catastrophe?' Unsafe play with atomic fire continues. The Hiroshima bomb is followed by the hydrogen bomb. In the same period of time man's moral stature grows little or not at all.

These men are not unique. We cite them as typical. They share the universally low ceiling of human wisdom on this point. Any suspicion that our leaders know how the necessary changes are to be brought about is quickly liquidated if we seriously look for unanimity among them as to specific procedures.

But why should one look to military, financial, or scientific leaders for a specific kind of expertness on peace? After all, Mr. MacArthur is a general occupied for a lifetime with war and war preparation. Mr. Baruch is a financier, Mr. Compton a physicist. Let us turn to Mr. Quincy Wright of the Department of International Relations at Chicago University. As only one symptom of Mr. Wright's accomplishments, he has developed a two-volume treatise on the history and problem of war. This treatise is based upon fifteen years of documentary research and constitutes an objective summary of data from a variety of fields—sociological, psychological, legal, historical, etc. A reading of this book indicates that Mr. Wright, who perhaps has as much right as any one to speak on the subject authoritatively, is quite humble about this authority and very much aware of his lack of adequate knowledge on the solution of the problem. In this treatise, one cannot gain the impression that Mr. Wright and his collaborators have found the necessary answers. Rather it becomes evident that the present writings of experts cannot be made to yield the answers. Our conclusion then is this: not only do men generally lack the know-how for peace, but there are as yet no experts who have the answer.

A third type of more direct consideration supporting the assumption that men do not now possess the know-how for peace, can be noted by a thoughtful observation of what our colleges and universities do, and do not, purport to teach. In the name of both professional and liberal education, they carry on vast programmes for teaching an enormous body of knowledge serving many types of human activity and social goal. We have schools for engineering, for medicine, for law, for art. We have no schools for peace. We have departments of literature, of economics, of geology, language and of education, and even of political science, but, with one exception,[1] there is to the writer's knowledge no institution of higher learning in the world which has seen fit to set up a department of peace. Discussions with college administrators and educational specialists seem to indicate a widespread agreement that there is no suitable body of subject matter sufficient to justify such a department. There are no textbooks that are suited and no instructors that are qualified for an appreciable number of courses suitable for such a department. In fact, the word 'peace' seems never to rate a five-letter space in a college catalogue.

Let us offer a slight semantic caution. The statement of our assumption is highly simplified. The discussion of it has been positive and somewhat dogmatic. Let us qualify. By 'lack of know-how', we mean *not enough knowledge*. We mean that, under the present complications of our world political situation and in the face of our psychological condition, we do not have the knowledge necessary to enable us to part company with the institution of organized human warfare. Our present knowledge is adequate neither to motivate the necessary sustained peace action

[1] Manchester College, North Manchester, Indiana, USA.

effort nor to give reasonable assurance of unanimity and success even if we were motivated. The probable quality and quantity of this aditional knowledge when it comes is not our problem here. How much effort, how many man hours of research it will require we cannot now say. It may be very great. We should be prepared to pay for it, whatever the price. In the second place, we do not mean to say that there is no other lack. Other things besides knowledge are needed, but knowledge of what precisely these things are and how to get them is tragically inadequate. It is not that we have no other requirements for peace; rather it is that, of all our needs, the need for greater understanding of what these requirements are deserves first place on our agenda of consideration and concern.

If the assumption be accepted that adequate peace know-how is not now in our possession, the immediate directive is obvious—namely, SEARCH. Out of the millions of human experiences over hundreds of generations, comes the generalized principle—when we don't know how to get what we want, we spend our time and devote our intellectual energies to finding out how to get it. But will this widely accepted common-sense principle be fearlessly applied to our present global political situation? This is the social situation. This is the social challenge. But, will it be accepted? Let us BEWARE! Our over-all diagnosis is not new. It has been made before. But adequate search has not happened.

In 1945 President Franklin D. Roosevelt said in his last prepared but not delivered speech, 'If men are to live together in peace and progress, it is essential that we develop a science of human relations.' In the years since they were uttered, these ringing words have been called to the attention of millions of readers and listeners. Why has so little been done about it? During this same time, the nation which he represented has contributed heavily toward the science of physical relations. Shortly after Mr. Roosevelt's death, Dr. Vannevar Bush, as Director of the U.S. Office of Scientific Research and Development, made a report which the President had requested several months previously. In Mr. Roosevelt's directive, the science of human relations was not specifically mentioned. Mr. Bush, in his report, Science the Endless Frontier, allotted no space to the problem of human relations. Two or three years later and after much debate, the United States Congress legislated into existence the National Science

Foundation. The question of providing explicitly for Social Science in the act was specifically considered and finally rejected. There is little reason to believe that the science of human relations has fared much better at the hands of the other nations.

One of the first research steps towards a science of peace could well be a very systematic and quantitative investigation into the cause of such delay or evasions as illustrated in the preceding paragraph. In the absence of and preliminary to such research data the tentative impressions of various observers should prove valuable. The author will therefore set forth his own generalizations resulting from several years of observation, inquiry, and reflection. For the time being their validity must rest mainly upon their appeal to the experience and logic of the reader. These generalizations, if corroborated by the conclusions of other observers, may be taken as working hypotheses until further data invalidate them, and better hypotheses supersede them. This discussion does not purport to be all-inclusive. We propose to suggest *some* of the ideational factors which blockade forthright decision for large-scale serious search for more adequate knowledge for war's eradication.

As in many other aspects of social psychology, the notions with which we have here to deal are in their most potent form vague and indistinct. They are, let us say, nine-tenths feeling and one-tenth thought. This makes them difficult to deal with. Possibly if we look carefully for the ideas that are implied and obscure, they can be smoked out and rendered harmless. As with any other science, it is the purpose of psychological science, especially in its early or philosophic stages, to struggle for added clarity.

Broadly speaking our unfavourable ideology has two aspects. On the one hand we overestimate the adequacy of our present knowledge and understanding, and on the other we underestimate the possibility of our gaining more adequate knowledge and understanding. Why search for something we don't need? Why search for something which cannot be found?

The Assumption that Present Knowledge is Adequate

One's lack of adequate knowledge is not likely to be cured as long as one is *unaware* of such lack of knowledge. Now, the assumption that we have no great need for more knowledge is seldom or never explicit. It is implicit in our words and actions, in our silences and in our inactions. If one scrutinizes the relevant discussions of our scientific, political, and educational leaders, such as those referred to above, one finds that they make no explicit mention of the lack of peace know-how. We would like to make this point more explicit by illustrating from the pronouncements of an intellectual leader for whom we have great respect. One of the most thrilling documents of our time is the essay by Norman Cousins, *Modern Man is Obsolete*. Perhaps in our enthusiasm over Mr. Cousins' extraordinary treatise, many of us were blind to what was left out. Mr. Cousins does not say how obsolescent man is to be remodelled or reconverted. He does indicate, along with Emery Reeves and a number of other writers, that a conversion of our political institutions is in order. Nationalism has a stranglehold on our psychology. But how do we get rid of it? If a writer of Mr. Cousins' depth and clarity doesn't say how this reform is to be brought about, are we not justified in assuming that he does not know? If he does not say that neither he nor others know, are we not justified in assuming that he is unaware that none of us know?

In conversations, in speeches, in writings, we find men coming again and again profoundly close to some of the crucial elements in our difficulty, such as lack of courage and morale, trust, and faith in one another. They seem always to stop short, however, of an exact recognition of the limitations of our present knowledge and understanding of the cause and cure of our fear, distrust and low morale. Even the most brilliant among our thinkers and writers are caught up in this widespread 'conspiracy of silence' regarding this most basically disastrous type of ignorance—the ignorance of ignorance. Awareness of ignorance is indispensable to the removal of ignorance. Let us recall Socrates' statement: 'The Delphian oracle hath said that I am the wisest of men. If this be true it is because I, of all men, know that I know not.'

Our blindness to blindness—our unawareness of ignorance—is partly facilitated by the awareness of present knowledge (which is partial and incomplete). Because we know something, we are liable to fall into the assumption that we know all or at least know enough. The facts we know are liable to crowd out of our consciousness the fact of our knowledge limitations.

There is often a misleading satisfaction to our partial answers, which causes us to overlook their incompleteness. In a recent nation-wide survey of opinion in the U.S.A., over 80 per cent of the sample population gave human greed as the cause of war. Let us assume this as a more or less valid answer. The common man seems to possess considerable realistic awareness of some of the crucial elements in human behaviour. Our awareness of greed, however, may blind us to the thought that neither the common man nor the uncommonly expert man knows either how to get rid of greed or how to get rid of war in spite of greed.

Many of the remedies for war might be labelled 'could-if' remedies. We *could* get rid of war *if* we could or would change our economic system, *if* we would practice the Golden Rule, *if* the nations would be willing to surrender a measure of their sovereignty, etc. While emphasizing one or another of these propositions, we overlook the need to know how to get the 'could-if' proposition developed into an actual operation. An important test of adequacy of knowledge comes at the point where it does or does not indicate practical and acceptable action. The blockading assumption that our present knowledge is adequate for peace, may best be removed by pointedly asking, just precisely what is the knowledge we have and what opportunity does this knowledge open up for realistic peace effort.

The Assumption that Better Knowledge is Not Obtainable

Escape from ignorance is further blocked by two short words: 'we can't'. One hears, 'Suppose it be admitted that we do not possess enough knowledge and understanding to achieve peace. This does not mean that we can get it. If we have no adequate tool with which to dig, why dig? If there be no such treasure in existence, why search?' And so on. In the last analysis it is up to the reader to choose between this 'practical' assumption and its opposite working assumption that for war and other conflict there *are* solutions and that human intelligence *is* capable of finding them.

The inapplicability of scientific intelligence to the problem of war seems based upon two wide-spread closely related lines of thought which we wish to challenge. One has to do with the nature of the problem. The other relates to the nature of science. Let us discuss these in this order.

As contrasted to problems of physical relations are the problems of human relations, by their nature, insoluble? Lack of faith in the power of human intelligence to solve life's problems is especially pronounced with respect to social problems. There is a wide-spread tendency to argue that human intelligence is suitable for solving only certain kinds of problems. A common expression is that scientific reasoning can further material but not spiritual progress. This gloomy position is supported by the explanation that problems in human relations are rendered insoluble by a distinct factor not present in problems of physical relations. This factor is referred to by a multitude of terms. In this chapter we are referring to it by the term, attitude. It involves all those situations where a heavy role is played by men's emotions or feelings—situations where human volition and decision are crucial. Let us turn now to some of the fallacies and confusions in this connection, which may be responsible for the lack of enthusiasm for a science of peace.

False Assumptions about Attitudes

There lurks in the minds of many men a false notion that human attitude cannot be comprehended by human reason. Since reasoning is the basis of scientific process, there can be no science of attitude or of anything in which attitude plays a large role. Many people contend explicitly that man-made science is neither suited nor suitable to take on the problem of adjusting human values. A great many people, obscurely but stubbornly, harbour the notion that our reasoning processes must always break down against the mystery of human motive and will.

Too often it happens that the more stress one lays on this mystery of attitude, the less time he seems to have for the proposition that our trouble is due to lack of knowledge. The rival formulation runs simply—'willingness and not knowledge is our need. Since men are not willing to use the knowledge they now have, why put our hope in more knowledge?'

Careful analysis of this type of erroneous thinking reveals three more or less distinguishable elements:

(*a*) Attitude, by its very nature, is unknowable. It is essen-

IDEOLOGICAL BLOCKADES TO A SCIENCE OF PEACE 67

tially an impenetrable mystery. Like the wind, it 'bloweth where it listeth and no one can tell whence it cometh'.

(b) A man's attitudes are unaffected by what he knows. Even if we could know ever so much more, our attitudes would remain unimproved by this new knowledge.

(c) Human intellect and reason are incapable of objectively coping with this subjective kind of reality. The irrational processes of pride and prejudice, hate and fear, lord it over the rational. Our emotions interrupt our reason, distort our conclusions and misdirect our research. Man intellectual is no match for man volitional and emotional.

Put all this together and the natural feeling is one of inhibiting fear to cope with a stupendous mass of subjective reality. Man has gradually left behind many stultifying fears. But more and more this particular fear stands out: man is afraid of himself. He is afraid of himself because he is afraid of his attitudes (his fears included). He is afraid of them because he doesn't understand them. He doesn't understand them because he hasn't the heart to face them boldly and reasonably.

This is crucial to further progress. It is no slip in logic to say that without a science of attitude there can be no science of social relations.

Now let us note that there is much fact about attitude which accounts for such wide-spread feeling against the possibility of such a science. One of the most obvious facts about attitude is that it is still much of a mystery. Man's attitudinal behaviour *is* an enigma—an enigma which the past 3,000 years of scholarly thinking and scientific research has not abolished. It is more realistic to admit than to deny the present mystery in why man wants what he wants when he wants it. From a limited point of view, the unknowability of man's emotional nature gets preliminary support when we honestly ask how much do we as yet know. The first impression of the casual inquirer, who is not satisfied with empty words and uncertain abstractions, is to feel that we are up against a blank and unyielding wall of ignorance. Only the dogmatic know the answers. Only the callous and the indifferent are content with the answers they get.

Human attitudes do show great resistance to logical assault. The most scientific data, the most objective evidence, seem so often to leave man's heavily habituated prejudices untouched.

Again and again, we meet with failure in our attempts to reason a man out of his basic values. But, worst of all, our emotions and our feelings do often bedevil and dominate our intellectual processes. Reason seems to have a way of falling overboard when strong emotion or passion arises. Even in moments of relative calm, our conclusions are distorted not only by conceptions with which we started, but by our initial or habitual feelings. Wishful thinking is universal. Our feelings and our wants dictate the direction of our thinking. Reason is a tool which we use to find out how to get what we want. If our wants are anti-social, the reasoning faculty will be used for anti-social ends.

How can we deal with this attitude that our attitudes are outside of the realm of reason and science? What antidote is there to the feeling that emotional man is unknowable, is impervious to knowledge, is incapable of achieving valid knowledge of his emotions in the face of their distracting influence? Since this attitude is blocking progressive thought and action toward the next best development in human destiny, how can we point out to reasonable men in their reasonable moments the elements of invalidity in this negative point of view?

Let us take up first the notion that there is something essentially mysterious about this very important aspect which we refer to by such terms as attitudinal, emotional, volitional, or spiritual or religious. Perhaps the most important antidote for this feeling of negation and despair is to change our terms slightly and emphasize the fact that we are here dealing with a kind of behaviour. Let us ask why and what is so incomprehensible about a man's behaviour when he behaves attitudinally, emotionally, volitionally, spiritually, or religiously. Surely this behaviour cannot be totally invisible or intangible, or we would not know enough about it to mention it. Any behaviour anywhere accessible to the human senses is an invitation to clearer observation and intensive study for purposes of further understanding.

Great progress has been made in the study of numerous kinds of behaviour. This includes the behaviour not only of such entities as planets and plants and animals, but includes also certain aspects of the behaviour of man himself. Inspiring is the progress in the past 300 years in the study of man's physiological behaviour. When we pass from man's physiological to his sociological behaviour, why do we have to become defeatists and assume that the causations and the consequences are inherently mysterious and beyond finding out?

We need here to challenge the dualism which says that man's world and man's nature are divided into two parts, the one characterized and the other not characterized by the principle of ascertainable and knowable cause and effect. As over against the notion that attitudinal man is unknowable, we again submit the alternative opinion that he is unknown because we have not made sufficient effort to find him out.

There is a popular notion often mentioned by the more cynical that human volition and motivation is 90 per cent or more emotional and 10 per cent or less intellectual. Whether this be true or the opposite, we can ill afford not to give our rational faculties a chance at the total problem of human behaviour. Rationality is suited to study that which is rational or that which is non-rational or even that which is irrational. Insanity itself is a suitable subject of study for the relatively more sane.

Anti-social attitudes are as natural as measles and mumps and, like measles and mumps, are not to be abolished by undisciplined anger and moralistic denunciation, but by appropriate means to be ascertained by objective study. Like the torrents of Niagara and Victoria and the floods of the Ganges and the Volga, they are controllable by intellectual man. Of course, human feelings and desires are an enigma to the human mind. But so are birth and death, the coming and going of the seasons, the rising and the setting of the sun. All presently solved problems were once unsolved and *apparently* impregnable.

Next, what shall we say about the notion that man in his prejudice is totally or practically impervious to logic and to information? We regard this as a faulty inference based upon partial evidence. In the first place, let us call attention to the widespread observation that attitudes do change. These changes are accompanied, in many instances, by an improved social relationship—an increased harmony. Moreover, these changes must have some cause. While this causation is at present incompletely understood, we do know that attitudes and knowledge interact continuously. It is a common observation that not only do feelings affect thinking and knowing, but thinking and knowing affect feelings.

Now, for newly acquired knowledge or information to have any particular effect upon a person's attitudes, it must be appropriate thereto. Give any man new and acceptable information about the unfriendly behaviour of a neighbour and his attitude is almost sure to change. The great fallacy frequently here is to expect a small bit of information, which fits acceptably into the attitudinal and intellectual pattern of the would-be persuader, to immediately nullify long-established emotional habits of the person he is trying to persuade. It is relatively easy to have in mind the things that we are trying to tell our neighbour. But it is likewise easy to overlook thousands of previous bits of information on which the neighbour bases his opinions or beliefs. Too often we are misled by the autocratic feeling within us that the other person must accept and act upon the information which we offer him. The democratic position would emphasize not only the right of individual, thoughtful choice, but also the right of access to relevant and adequate knowledge.

Let us turn now to the feeling that the human intellect is incapable of conquest over that feature of behaviour which of itself so often interrupts, distorts, and misdirects our intellectual operations. Of course, there are stages of anger and of fear which paralyse or derange the intellectual process. There are times when we make every effort to think of the words which can express and the arguments which can justify our enmity or our partiality to one or another person. But this is not the whole story. Emotions have their ebb and flow. Moreover, they differ from person to person. This gives reason its chance. Great intellectual feats of hydraulic engineering have been accomplished by some men while others were struggling desperately to save their properties and their lives from surging floods. Division of labour and extensive co-operation can be practised in the intellectual conquest of human emotion. Arrangements can be made to give sincere men the leisure and protection from emotional pressure to do the research necessary to find out how to get competition and antagonism under reasonable control and confined to safer limits or channels. Human intelligence, both at the personal and group level, can learn the art of self-defence against unfortunate emotional pressure.

Now let us look directly at that part of the argument which is disdainful of intelligence because of the fact that intelligence is a tool whose use is determined by our motives. It is because of this fact that we insist that science needs to be redirected. If science is to save instead of destroy, it must somehow come under a better set of motivations. The motive of curiosity is not enough. Other motives are increasingly operating—some positive and some negative. The cure for bad use of reasoning is to be found in better use. Wherever there are those who deprecate the fact that men are developing their wits to make weapons, there is the challenge to develop the wit to bring about peace.

The tragedy is that our love is too much unlighted by reason and our reason too often unsponsored by love. Only by false assumption are we required to discard either intelligence or sympathy. Love and intellectuality can be characteristics of one and the same act. Love and reason can be and frequently are lined up on the same side and in the same enterprise. If we are told that the spirit of antagonism can enlist intelligence, our reply is that so too can co-operation. Reason can serve love as well as hate. If we are to survive, it *must serve love* instead of hate.

The love of humanity says our goal is human betterment; reason can say, let's find out how to achieve it.

Greatest of all, this opportunity of marriage or merger between love and reason can be reproductive, generative, dynamic, and creative. Reason can, by love, be enlisted to find out how we can generate more love. Obviously, the cynic is correct when he argues that there is so much hate in the world and so little love. At least functionally, this is correct, but the amount of positive emotion in operation need not be fixed and unchangeable. Surely if love or desire to co-operate has any reality about it at all, it has its antecedents or its causes. Why not look for these? Human intelligence has been fabulously successful in finding out how to generate electricity; why should we assume that there is no way to find out how to generate love? We live in a world of trillions of watts of power. Such power would constitute no hazard in a world of friendly men. We need to use our intellectual processes on the commodity of friendliness—to seek out the secrets of its origin and development. If this can be done, the process of reason and science will be seen to be, not the alternative to love, but its aid and ally.

Possibly the reader may feel by now that we are overemphasizing the concept of love. In this, our thinking has been based on a widely accepted generalization that positive and friendly fellow-feelings are essential to greater harmony and to peace. This is just one approach. If it be false or inadequate, only careful study will be able to reveal it. If and as the need for something else becomes apparent, we can plan our research to discover what this something else is.

There is another approach to this dilemma of misdirection of our intelligence by our wants and motives. This is in the interaction btween our wants and our knowledge. Human wants are never more elastic, more changeable, more dynamic than under optimal conditions of interaction with human reason and knowledge. The nature of his personality makes a man struggle not only to satisfy his wants or wishes but to improve them. The oft noted observation that an individual 'does not want what he wants when he gets it' is significant and understandable. The changed attitude results from the new knowledge that the sought and achieved goal does not yield what it previously was thought to yield. Few, if any, of the things we want stand alone or in isolation or as final ends in themselves. Each maintains its meaning in relation to other parts of the pattern of wishes. The order of the priority and the relation of these parts, and hence of the total pattern, change constantly. For the most part, we spend our days not in getting what we want but in getting that which will enable us to get what we want. This is to say that most of our ends or goals are really means to more final or more eventual ends or goals. The role of reason and of knowledge is in determining appropriate means to more eventual ends. It has been aptly said that men do not want war but that they want what causes war. It may even be said that they want what war causes. Better knowledge of these causes and of more desirable alternatives might quickly change their behaviour.

The interrelation and the interaction between wants and wants, between ends and means, is inescapable. In this complex interaction, reason and knowledge play an indispensable role. Change in consciousness of relation is primarily affected by new knowledge or frequently, if you prefer, by new insights. The Kellogg-Briand Pact purported to encourage nations to reject war as a national policy, that is, as a means towards nationally desired ends. It is reasonable to say that the treaty was ineffectual because knowledge of a better means to the desired ends did not exist. Ask any patriot today about the disarmament of his nation and he will demand to know the alternative to armament. Ask the diplomats to work for multilateral disarmament and they will ask you not only for the means for bringing about this end, but also the means for bringing about the ends for which they conceive armament to be the means. Adequate knowledge of relationship is necessary for valid judgment. To pass judgment on action, even one's own, without adequate knowledge is to risk error and injustice. What greater risk of error can there be than in the failure to make all necessary and possible effort to achieve necessary and achievable knowledge?

If men then, in getting what they want, get war also which they do not want, we have clearly a job waiting for our intellect. Human intelligence (especially at the scientific level) has the function of separating the wanted and the unwanted. In the matter of drink and food, we have gradually and progressively succeeded in separating the wholesome from the unwholesome. In a complex social setting it is difficult to know always which of our alternative opinions and values will contribute most and least to the perpetuation of war or the promulgation of peace. Give men and nations a more certain and more economical means of achieving what they want and they will 'buy' it out of the logic of economy.

Is something besides knowledge needed to abolish war? Yes! Something besides knowledge was needed to abolish yellow fever. A hundred years ago we did not know what this was. We did not then know that we needed to eradicate the anopheles mosquito. Research was needed to find this out. What besides knowledge is needed to abolish war? We do not now know, but we do need the faith to find out and the decision to use our energy to do the research necessary to find out.

If the pessimist thinks the job of social understanding is difficult and the optimist thinks it is easy, then the former is right and the latter is wrong. Let us not underestimate the size of the job. Pragmatic optimism requires that we think in terms of co-operation among thousands or millions of intellects. The only thing that can save us is some cumulative method of research and co-ordination of researchers which will enable us to stand on each other's intellectual shoulders to achieve the necessary reach. This is the principle which stands out clearly in the record of science to date. But are we willing to trust our intelligence to the scientific method? Are we willing to surrender ourselves to the scientific attitude? And merge it with the will to live and to love? Into our world of knowledge, power-producing information regarding atoms flows faster and faster. It flows very much faster than harmony-producing information regarding attitudes. Why? Because the method and the tool of science is being abundantly used in one field and not in the other. Are we willing to make arrangements for its rapid use in the field of attitude? Why do we hesitate? Let us now look into some of our notions of the nature of science which may be responsible for this delay.

Misconceptions and Prejudices Regarding Science

It is the writer's contention that the resistance to the adequate utilization of the scientific process in the realm of social relations is due to a negative attitude based upon inadequate conception of what science is and upon unjustified prejudices against its essential nature. Revision of our ideas about science is necessary for the revision of our attitudes toward science. We will organize our discussion under seven separate questions.

Is Science Merely Physical?

A very serious part of our prejudicial attitude toward science is found in that incomplete conception which makes science and physical science synonymous. Here we have an error which is easy to explain. It is easier to look at the products of science than to look at the process. Its most obvious products to date are physical. Science has produced an enormous number of gadgets —hundreds of millions of radio and TV sets, electric fans and refrigerators, telephones, automobiles, and aeroplanes. One of Alexander Graham Bell's first messages over his telephone was, 'See what God hath wrought'. The more we look, the more we see what the God of Science hath wrought in terms of physical instruments. This way of looking at science has frequently been denounced as too materialistic or too utilitarian. Science should, however, be given great credit for its physical and material contributions. It is accurate and realistic to note the profound effects on raising the economic standard of living and the standard of health, including increase in life expectancy and decrease in mortality from certain types of disease.

IDEOLOGICAL BLOCKADES TO A SCIENCE OF PEACE 75

However, all this still provides too narrow a notion of what the contribution of science can be. To evaluate science for the purpose of its future guidance, it is necessary to look not only at its more obvious products, but even more to the basic elements of the process by which the products are made possible. Greater emphasis needs to be placed upon the scientific method or scientific attitude. It is incorrect to assume that because the chief practical products of science have been physical instruments for faster transportation, wider communication, and brighter illumination, it therefore is not suited to produce, through better techniques of education, economics, or politics, more love, more co-operation, more harmony. Unless science can do the latter as well as the former, it will justify the appellation of a false Messiah. It cannot eventually fulfil its promise to ever greater physical comfort and gratification, unless the threat from spiritual or attitudinal conflict is abated. Life expectancy has been increased through scientific physical sanitation but is being threatened by the social disease called war. Political sanitation, like physical, will have to be achieved by the appropriate dedication of organized human intelligence to determining relevant cause and cure. Even now life expectancy is still very low for three-fourths of the world's population because of the inadequacy of mere physical science. The extreme physical nature of the interests and objectives of most of those who engage in and promote science is accidental and incidental and is not inherent in the scientific method *per se*.

Is Science Infallible?

A second block to the reordering of science inheres in the feeling among many that science does not need to be reordered because science is innocent and blameless and incapable of misorderly behaviour. There are many persons who enjoy the assumption that science is a quest for pure truth and hence its goals and its directions are not to be questioned. To protect this comfortable position, they resist and reject any such indictment as that presented in Chapter IV. The true perspective must be that of those who feel that science is neither a sacred cow nor uniformly a villain or irremediably a Frankenstein monster. It is extremely important that we evaluate science accurately and take it for what it is worth and encourage it and promote it when and where it is worthy. If this means admitting that there are unworthy and undesirable developments, we must face it courageously and act decisively for correction. One phrase frequently heard from the apologists for science is that it is not science that is at fault but the uses which are made of scientific findings or products. This does not go deep enough. More and more we will have to come to grips with the objectives of science and evaluate and be willing to criticize the kind of findings which are aimed at. More and more we should be willing to amplify the statement and say that not science in the abstract is at fault, but the uses which we make not only of scientific *knowledge* but also of scientific *research*. Let us admit that we have made an astounding error in using the scientific method to release prematurely an unsafe amount of power into a conflict-prone world. There is then no logic to the contention that we have to continue this error.

Is Science Dangerous?

In addition to the misconception that science is essentially limited to physical problems and the feeling that it is necessarily infallible, there are a number of distinctly negative prejudices against science, which discourage its extensive application to social problems. These prejudices include the charges that it is dangerous, unpredictable, amoral, undemocratic, and inhumane. Some of these notions rest in part upon realistic observation of what has actually happened. They are partially supported by incontrovertible evidence. But conclusions based upon these observations are often false, being coupled with the assumption that the science of tomorrow must contain all the shortcomings of the science of yesterday. Let us not spend undue time maligning science because of its errors. Too often we yield to the dangerous impulse to throw out the baby with the bath. True, it is overdue for a good scrubbing. But we need not live without it. Neither need we live so dangerously with it if we have the courage and the perspective to make appropriate changes in it.

Thus far in this book, we have been supporting the idea that our present horrifying predicament is largely science-born. The feeling then is natural and legitimate and realistic not only that science can be and is dangerous, but also that it can become much more dangerous than it now is. The erroneous assumption, however, is that science *has* to be dangerous—that there is no way to control it. The antidote for this fallacy must reside somehow in the forthright position that science will be what we make it; that its future can be held in the hands of thoughtful and responsible men and not left in the merciless lap of the gods. We must remember that not only is there such a thing as dangerous inopportune knowledge but also dangerously inappropriate ignorance. An unhappy mixture of the two can be worse than either alone. This latter is increasingly the lot of modern man. It is a false and cowardly position which says that man shall have nothing to say about what the next new knowledge shall be. It is intellectual treason to acquiesce in the position that, for any given point in the history of a race or an individual, one body of knowledge is as much needed or as safe as any other. Why here, of all places, do men dull their sense of personal and social discrimination and responsibility?

However, the concept of responsibility for science's future is inseparable from the concept of control. Is the possibility of control of science theoretically sound? This question, as well as the perplexing question about the amoral nature of science is inseparable from the question of the *predictability* of outcome of scientific research.

Is Science Predictable?

Can science be predicted? Against the notion that it cannot, we must move carefully. It has been impressive to the writer to meet both friend and enemy of science on the same wrong side of this issue. To support this notion of unpredictability of science, it is argued that science is a creative enterprise powered by the motive of curiosity. The life dominated by creative curiosity must be allowed to follow whatever leads develop and to stick to the truth regardless of where it leads. Science by its very nature is an adventure of great uncertainty of outcome. It is argued that the scientist has to be free to follow his own spontaneous impulses. Any submission to extraneous pressures will result in his perpetuating human fallacies and biases.

In unpredictability, as in other fallacies, we are confronted with a half-truth supported by facts of the past. It is a highly significant fact that science *has been* unpredicted in its outcome. No one, one hundred years ago, did predict the present-day dangerous combination of scientific development and political condition. Pasteur and his contemporaries had scant or no appreciation of the spectre of bacteriological warfare. But human prediction grows out of human experience. The more experience we have with scientific method and procedure, the more we should become able to anticipate its most essential effects. The limitations of judgment of Francis Bacon need not be the limitations of men who have back of them the record of three hundred years of scientific history including a half dozen decades of interaction between science and politics and economics.

The modern philosopher of science is now in a position not only to ask how did the scientific method happen to develop, but, what is more significant, how it happened to be applied (or misapplied) first in the area of lesser need and greater danger. As with cultural development in general, so with science, we herein challenge the assumption that that which has happened is the only thing which could have happened. From here on, we can try to make better and better judgments as to which scientific directions need most to be supported in the interest of harmony and safety as over against power and catastrophe.

We believe that there has been an overstress on the principle of serendipity (i.e., finding something you aren't looking for). Its validity is limited. True, Columbus did discover America when he was looking for India, but this was not a discovery outside the realm of navigation and geography. Relatively and directly, it had little to do with problems in such fields as metallurgy or bacteriology.

What we find depends in part upon where we look. If our troubles are political, we must look into politics or closely related areas. Theorizers about science frequently make great use of prediction as the one outstanding criterion for distinguishing science from non-science. The ultimate proof of the scientific validity of a formula comes when the scientist can say, 'We were able to predict the outcome'. What a fatal piece of irony for us all if the outcome of the predictive enterprise itself continues unpredictable.

We may not find it fitting to criticize basic scientists—men like Einstein, Rutherford, Chadwick, Bohr, Meitner—for not having had either the time or the ability to predict the atomic bomb. This does not mean, however, that nothing can be done about fundamental principles for guiding society or scientists in the choice of scientific direction in the future. Predictions do not have to be absolute or infallible to be useful. The principle of probability can be used *about* science as well as *in* science. Science is an enterprise which involves decisions at many levels. To the extent that prediction becomes impossible, decision becomes a myth. Science is responsible for a tremendous increase in man's confidence in his ability to control his own destiny. We recommend that this confidence be extended to include the resolution to control science itself.

Is Science Amoral?

One of the confusions resulting (in part) from an overemphasis upon the unpredictable nature of science is represented in the phrase that science is amoral. This would seem to take scientific behaviour out of the realm of ethics. We believe this notion has done a distinct disservice to the cause of human betterment through science. Social responsibility leaves off when and where we are unable to predict consequences in terms of goodness or badness, advantage or disadvantage to people. This notion seems to be responsible for much of the coldness towards introducing science into human relations. In fact, there seems to be considerable antipathy between moral and scientific philosophers. Many of the latter have little use for the phrases which include the term moral. This is not the place to clear up this misunderstanding. We believe, however, that both the moralists and the antimoralists have slipped a cog because of the assumption about our inability to foresee the social consequences of scientific research. Recently in a sectarian journal, we found the sentence, 'Science is not evil but some of its results are'. This seems to ignore a widely accepted principle of judging a vine by its fruits. Here, as elsewhere, it is implied not that the effects of science are neither good nor bad, but that, to the contrary, they are both good and bad. Why not then say that science is both moral and immoral? This does less violence to pragmatic truth than to say it is neither.

Scientific research or the scientific pursuit of knowledge as well as the use of knowledge is an activity. It consists of definite acts following deliberate choice or decision. The moral quality of an act depends upon the total situation in which it is committed. An important aspect of the research situation is in the probable uses of the discovery. If these probabilities are 'bad' the activity leading to the discovery would seem to be 'bad'. Any discovery which leads to the extinction of the human species would be considered by most of us an unfortunate discovery. To pursue such a discovery knowingly would then be considered unwise. To the statement that knowledge (or truth) is 'good' can be added 'yes, some knowledge, perhaps most, but not all'.

It has been suggested that acting in a situation where one cannot foresee the outcome may in itself constitute an immoral piece of behaviour. As a matter of fact, the moral or social justification for scientific research is basically maintained on the assumption that it is likely to do more good than harm. Recent scientific and political developments cast increasing doubt upon this assumption. One aspect of morality or social responsibility is included in the notion that a man is not to blame if he has no alternative. Our suggestion is that there is an alternative to the science which more and more obviously gives us more and more power which is more and more dangerous. This alternative is to turn our attention and our support to science which aims at more harmony to make more safe present and future power.

Is Science Amenable to Social Control?

A fourth prejudice against science, sometimes difficult to recognize, is in the thought somehow that it is not amenable to popular control. Between the lines we can read the notion that science is something which cannot be guided by the will or wish of the people. The democratic humanism within many of us rebels against science on this score. It is assumed that the scientist does not and, by right, ought not to take orders from anyone; that is, as a scientist. Least of all can he listen to the common people. They are too uninformed and uninterested in the erstwhile actualities of his enterprise. Here is a stubborn position which we have found defended by scientists and laymen, both by friend and non-friend of science. Again we say it is partly true and partly untrue, partly defensible and partly indefensible. It makes a difference whether we are talking about the over-all goal of the scientific operation or whether we are thinking about the technical details of the operation. This is true in any division of labour, especially expert labour.

Why should anyone assume that it is none of the public's business what the scientist produces? After all, this is the people's world and science is doing things to it. Now one aspect of the stubborn position against the democratizability of science is in the concept of science needing to be pure—the scientist needing to be free. This includes the idea that the only legitimate motivation for the scientist is curiosity, where knowledge is pursued purely for the sake of knowledge. Any non-curiosity motivation is thought to be some kind of desecration. Many scientists, as many artists, seem to entertain a strong prejudice against the word utilitarian. Much of our trouble on this score is that our attitudes now operate on the basis of habits of thought and feeling originated in the dawn hours of science. Recently there has been going on, outside and around the ivory tower of pure science, an ocean of events which has shaken the tower to its foundations. In so many places, we see science baking bread and hewing wood and drawing water. It is often contended that science cannot thrive or operate at all under dictatorship. This idea will have to be revised. Behold, at present, a raft of dictators telling scientists what to work on. The big question is, who will dictate—the few or the many? Of course, science is now widely accepted as highly useful and effective. 'Useful to whom?' and 'Effective for what?' are vital questions. 'Knowledge for what?' is a question which we have ignored too long and too much, in both scientific and educational circles. Science is today enormously supported and highly guided by motives of utility, but they are in dangerous measure unfortunately partisan.

Daily it becomes true in more places that science is for sale to the highest bidder. It is for hire by those most quick to appreciate its potency. These seem to be those of most partisan motives, those who sense the need for more power in the power struggle. Research institutions which acquiesce in this trend seem to grow more powerful. Those which do not acquiesce seem to grow less powerful.

The horror of Orwell's *1984* is spreading. The cure for our present dilemma is not merely social science, but democratic social science. Our legitimate goal is now science not only of and for people, but by the people (through the people's agents). In this process, not only would the scientist be asking the people what they want science to achieve, but the support for science, both moral and financial, would come from the people. To attempt to protect mankind defensively from science by denunciation and by negation of any sort is to engage in a losing battle. We recommend the faith that science can be democratically controlled and still be science. What is more, it can become safe for democratic man.

Can Science Be Humane?

A fifth prejudice against science is related to science's well-deserved reputation for being highly dispassionate. In order to arrive, a scientist must be minimally swayed by personal emotion. He must not allow himself to be deflected by personal sympathy. The truth he seeks must not exclude the truth that hurts. We have already said that science can be democratic. We have said that the scientist does not have to be unsympathetic to human wishes in choosing the more final ends toward which he will organize his scientific work. But this prejudice which we are here discussing relates to the heartlessness of the scientist in the daily process of his research. It is said that he is unsympathetic to the rights of the material which he uses; treating them not as ends in themselves, but as means in finding out whatever it is he wants to find out. He is said to be ruthless and emotionally indifferent toward that which he is observing and manipulating. His touch is a cold and heartless one. If he needs to destroy in order to analyse, he seems to have no compunction. This may be all right with inanimate material, but not with humans. Who cares what happens to a few million molecules or a billion bacteria? We have plenty and to spare. That we begin to feel differently, however, when it comes to animal life is illustrated in the long-standing battle between some of the scientists and the anti-vivisectionists. When we approach the level of human personality, the issue becomes extremely acute. As one humanistic educator said of a behaviouristic psychologist, 'Let him keep his unholy hands off matters that are personal and sacred'. At one time in the United States, there were a number of schools that were called by their patrons experimental. These labels have disappeared. Too often was the cry heard, 'I don't want my child made an experiment of'.

This feeling rests in part upon a profound sense of respect for the individual. This respect in turn must be respected. Respect for personality, however, must be intelligent and enlightened. It has a positive as well as a negative aspect. Disregard and vital neglect of an object is an extreme form of disrespect. If children are too sacred for ruthless experimenting upon, they are also too sacred to suffer the accidents and tragedies of ignorance and guess-work of parents and other educators. There is no greater aspect of respect than in serious effort to understand. The astronomer has come to understand the heavenly bodies, including a great deal of their inner composition. This is without the slightest interference with their operation or essential rights as suns and planets. What is true of the astronomer is true of the physiologist and can be true of the psychologist, sociologist, and political scientist. Much of present natural science does not demand or allow outright experiment. Moreover, let us not emphasize too much the idea that experiment requires manipulation and that manipulation must precede understanding. The ideal still rings true that we would first understand people as well as things nonpersonal before we start manipulating or even prescribing or recommending. If social science has been unduly awkward and inept in this respect, this may be due to uncritically copying from physical science, not only form, but an attitude of insensitivity to materials. This does not have to continue. We can learn to invent techniques which combine toughmindedness and tenderheartedness in our quest for the truth about human behaviour.

Conclusion

The health of nations and of individuals requires that we face these facts about science, the facts of its past achievements and its present deficiencies, the facts of what it can do to crush and what it can do to elevate mankind. We must accept the evidence of physical science, but not close the door on social science. We must face and admit the dangers; neither underestimate the terrifying possibilities nor flee from their presence. We must accept the difficulties of predicting scientific outcome, but we must not shut our eyes to the necessities of using an appreciable amount of our intelligence and scientific time in the interest of the best possible prediction at each successive level of scientific outlook. We must give human sympathy its best chance to be scientific and we must give human science a chance to be sympathetic. We must accept the challenge that science, like art, religion, and government, requires democratization. In science as in other matters we must not waver if we find that 'the price of freedom is eternal vigilance'.

We must face the fact that a terrible error has been made, that in a world crying for bread there have been thrown the stones of military weapons. We must recognize that through our scientific ingenuity, we have fostered the deadly scorpion of an armament race while hundreds of millions of children are denied their right to an egg or some milk. However, every true criticism against science argues not against science as it can be, but against science as it is. They argue not that we should abolish, but that we should reorder science. The 'all-powerful method of science' does not have to continue to 'give us the right things in the wrong order'.

As we cannot count on the infallibility of science, so we dare not count on the inevitability of progress. We dare not assume that our present knowledge is adequate. On the other hand, we need not assume that human intelligence has reached its limits of enlightenment. The closeness of man to himself need not prevent man from understanding man. The fact that there are attitudinal or spiritual aspects to man's nature can be no final argument against the progressive understanding of man's social behaviour. Both the difficulty and the urgent importance of understanding attitudinal and other aspects of social conflict and harmony argue for scientific method and procedure and for scientific faith. Have we the faith? Have we the will to believe in that which our best reason tells us is our best hope for peace and survival?

6
ARTICLES OF FAITH

New faith is greatly needed. If we are to extricate ourselves from the inertia which ties us to our present predicament, if we are to achieve the knowledge necessary to reorganize our society, if we are to catch up to our greater power with comparably greater harmony, if we are to overcome our present prejudices against a science of peaceful human relations, we will have to develop an appropriate and common pattern of faith. Such development requires a considerable amount of interaction among a considerable number of concerned individuals. As one contribution to such interaction, we wish in this chapter to present a formulation of a minimal platform of belief.

In what is here presented, there is no claim for originality with respect to the separate elements. All men display these elements to some extent at some time. If the reader is at all surprised, it will be in the combination. Broadly and simply speaking, these elements can be represented by the two familiar terms: science and democracy. It is our distinct impression that these two vital ideals have not been sufficiently closely associated. It is our conviction that herein lies the clue to our difficulty. Democracy without science is stupidity. Science without democracy is insanity.

There are five features to the faith we advocate.

1. The *goal*: Faith in human harmony (in the achievability of an unprecedented degree of harmony among the members of the human race).

2. The *means*: Faith in facts (in the procurability of facts relevant and indispensable to greatly enhanced harmony).

3. The *tool*: Faith in human intelligence (in the enormous power of human intelligence to progressively discover facts essential to increased human harmony).

4. The *method*: Faith in science (that the principles underlying scientific method and attitude are as applicable to the problems of human as to those of non-human relationships).

5. The *motive*: Faith in democratic or humanistic motivation (in the actual and potential existence of a sufficient amount of the motive of universal welfare—regard for mankind as a whole—to motivate a science of peace immediately, and eventually a science of human harmony in general).

Let us now present these five articles one by one. Under each article of faith, we shall endeavour to make clear what it is we need to live by and why, the difficulties confronting such faith, and the conditions needed for its growth.

ARTICLE 1. THE GOAL—FAITH IN THE ACHIEVABILITY OF HUMAN HARMONY

We believe that men everywhere want to live and to live more abundantly. Men want to save their lives and to make them more worth saving. This requires freedom. Freedom requires harmony. Only harmonious purposes can be free for fulfilment. Purposes in conflict are hampered and frustrated purposes. Freedom and fulfilment require the progressive elimination of conflict. For this two alternatives are open—to extinguish or adjust our purposes. Greater faith in the latter is greatly needed.

A faith fit for survival must include the sincere and dynamic belief that human purposes are modifiable and adjustable to a degree thus far unachieved; and this without violence, physical or psychological. The long-standing notion that, to be free, men have to fight it out (however natural) is an aberration of human sanity. The faith needed is a faith to supplant the vicious doctrine that freedom is something one has to *die* for. This faith says that ways can be found to *live* for freedom if we take the trouble to search. It rejects the philosophy that men have to choose between violence and slavery. As it is a faith that life can eventually be lived without violence and without the threat of annihilation, it further insists upon the rapid elimination of the notion that harmony is to be achieved by fear—military, economic, religious, political, or otherwise. Men need to live by the positive doctrine that the major portion of human conflict can be eradicated—without human frustration and desecration—that greater and better ways of co-operation can eventually be found.

Such a faith as here contemplated must be maintained against heavy odds. The fact of conflict is all about us. The pages of history run red with the record of human conflict carried on with some of the greatest display of human cunning. No major culture is known fully devoid of elements of the philosophy and even idealization of human conflict and violence. Heroism and bloodshed are tied close in the romantic mind of man. One of the most impressive and oppressive facts of our time is the fact of conflict.

For thousands of years, man has disappointed himself in his ethical ideals. He is confronted as he contemplates his history with a sickening amount of hypocrisy and insincerity surrounding his protestations of brotherhood. In spite of all our poetry about the law of love, we still see basically, underneath, the operation of the law of tooth and claw. The pages of history are filled with the crimes committed in the name of patriotism and brotherhood.

But this need not be the end of the story. Human life and human nature are capable of more than the gross behaviour now resulting from our total pattern of motive and attitude. Let us say, the ugly conglomerate of unrefined nature furnishes the elementary pigments from which a beautiful picture can be drawn. This, however, requires selectivity and an artistic or intelligent procedure of emphasis. The diabolical in man can be discouraged, the sympathetic can be encouraged. Man is neither saint nor demon, but, to an appreciable degree, a creature of culture and circumstance. This is no time to denounce the creature. While time remains, let us concern ourselves with the circumstances.

On the brighter side, it can be pointed out that human harmony (as well as conflict) is already a fact. A vast amount of harmonious interaction now takes place. How else could billions of humans even up to now exist upon such a rapidly 'shrinking' planet? Up to now, we have survived in the face of considerable power suited for mutual destruction. Our misfortune is not that we have no harmony; it is that we do not have enough. It does not grow fast enough. The tragedy is not that there is no opportunity for harmonizing. The tragedy is that our opportunities for greater power have been grasped with vigour, while the opportunities for purpose fulfilment through purpose harmonization have been neglected.

Just a word on what this faith is not. This is not a faith that harmony will come among men without human effort or by the accident of history, or in the face of our present ignorance. Utopian pictures have been drawn in the past. Brilliantly, men have drawn up elaborate codes of ethics with a profound vision of human brotherhood. They have left us frustrated. Apparently something essential has been missing.

Crucial among the missing pieces have been pieces of information. Ignorance of how harmony is to be achieved can be fatal. Logically therefore, article one of our faith cannot stand alone. To believe in the achievability of human harmony requires a belief in the discoverability of the necessary knowledge—knowledge of how this harmony is to be achieved—knowledge not now completely possessed by mankind. Therefore, let us turn to our second article.

Article 2. The Means—Faith in Facts

Knowledge is essential wherever man is the master of his own fate. Effective and satisfactory living requires understanding. This in turn requires knowledge. Knowledge requires facts. The discovery and use of facts requires faith—faith in their discoverability and their usefulness.

The role of knowledge in the solution of human problems is universal. If we take a broad view of human experience, the general principle is clear. Observations on it are so common that we are prone to lose awareness of their significance. Again and again we say in effect, when facing a difficulty, 'I wish I knew how to solve this problem'. After each such statement we may personally default without awareness of the penalty, but whether we evade the issue or whether we invest in further reflection or consult experts and special treatises or whether we engage in downright original research, we have by these words underscored for the billionth time human testimony to the handicap of human ignorance.

This universal fact is more dramatically incorporated in the broad history of human society. While it may be said that man's biological evolution has come about without assistance of human knowledge, this cannot be said about his sociological or cultural evolution. It is impossible to point to a single major step in human progress that has not come about as a result of something discovered or invented by the human mind. No real human problem has met its real solution without the discovery of some new fact.

Now, reverence for the facts already discovered is not the same as reverence for facts yet to be discovered. Preoccupation with the fruits of previous research might well stand between us and the facts yet to be discovered. What is needed is gratitude for what we have, coupled with a profound sense of its inadequacy. We should be able to say that what we have is but a token of that which we have a right to expect.

The faith in facts here called for is a belief in an inexhaustible reservoir from which new knowledge can be continuously drawn by the creative mind of man. It is an assumption that what we have is but a drop in the ocean compared with what there is yet to get. Surely there is no logic anywhere for assuming that man's intellectual history has now reached the point where further facts are undiscoverable. Everything in the history of human intellect points to the opposite. The more we have, the faster we can get more. Knowledge furnishes the instrumentation for securing more knowledge.

In spite of the evidence, the tensions on this faith are tremendous. We need a faith in facts, their potency and discoverability, to sustain us in the face of the delays, the frustrations, and even the insults with which we are incessantly met when we knock at the door of truth. One difficulty in sustaining this faith is confusion regarding supposed alternatives. There is the always-present notion that there is something else we need besides or even more than knowledge. It is of high importance to point out that the doctrine of the acute need for more facts is not necessarily a contradiction of the truth of other statements about what is needed for world peace and human harmony. Rather, it is an argument for the incompleteness of our present insights regarding these other needs. If, for instance, we say that war is caused by human greed or economic conflict, our faith is that we can come to know more about the cause and effect of these factors. If our formula for peace is more love or world government or technical assistance, we need more knowledge about where and how more love is to be brought about, how world government is to be made a reality, and how technical assistance can be made appreciably more than a passive verbalism or a political plaything or a salve to soothe the social conscience in countries disproportionately prosperous. To say we need knowledge to get peace is to say we need to know what it is that is needed for peace and how these needs can be realized. To say we know when we don't know is tragic. To know we don't know but to have no faith in our ability to learn or discover the knowledge is likewise tragic. Knowledge is not the substitute for the other needs. It is the prerequisite.

There is a very widespread observation that 'wars are caused by misunderstanding'. This observation is good but partial, and does us no good if we lack the faith for further search. We need to know what the misunderstandings are. The cure for misunderstanding is understanding. The antidote for fallacy is fact. A faith suitable for survival must include a working belief that for our misunderstandings there is waiting for us potential information regarding certain relevant facts even though no one can at the moment tell us specifically what these facts are.

This notion of war being caused by misunderstanding is sometimes denied. Certain persons confronting the appalling facts of power politics are tempted to say that there is an alternative and more realistic conception. They prefer to say that 'war is due to conflict of interest'. We suggest that these two concepts are not contradictory. Conflict of interest may very well be due to misunderstanding. But whatever the cause of conflict, how can we hope for readjustment unless we understand the conflict and its causation better? Call it conflict of interest—conflict of purpose —conflict of attitude—what you will. It is after all a maladjustment or a sickness which afflicts our society. Faith in facts for eliminating war can take its cue from the record of cures for other ills. Many medical cures have been made possible by medical knowledge and understanding. Others are anticipated. Why not anticipate cures for political ailment by political knowledge and understanding?

Now, a word on what this faith in facts is not. It is not a blind faith in the potency of promiscuous knowledge. It is not a faith merely in knowledge in general or knowledge for knowledge's sake. Just any knowledge on any subject will not suffice. Our human stockpile of knowledge has grown more in the last fifty years than in all previous history, but how tragic and unsatisfactory. Our faith in facts must be faith in facts appropriate to our needs.

This faith in appropriate facts, however, is incomplete without faith in an appropriate tool adequate for their discovery as well as use.

Article 3. The tool—Faith in Human Intelligence

For lifting ourselves out of our ignorance, we have, as Stuart Chase once pointed out, 'nothing to save us but our naked intelligence'. Faith in our intelligence furnishes the indispensable element for an indispensable type of action which we may refer to as research action. The facts needed are not to be waited for. They are to be achieved by human effort, by human ingenuity. They are not to be achieved by some 'sixth' or rare sense, but through the attribute of intelligence using the commonly recognized five senses we now have and processing the data which these senses furnish. This powerful and creative tool has worked wonders in physical matters. Why not trust it to dig up the facts needed for solving social problems? Progress requires not only confidence in the human mind as the tool for discovering pragmatic information but also as an adequate instrument for using knowledge after it is discovered. We have the capacity for making use not only of facts we now know but also of a much greater body of knowledge.

Too much stress has been laid, in certain circles, on the finiteness of the human mind. Whatever we may say about past and present limitations, there is sound sense in saying that these limits are temporary and hence extendable. There are at least three respects in which human intellectual limits are not fixed:

1. Acquisition of new knowledge can be unending—it seems unnecessary to assume a point beyond which mankind will not be discovering new facts.

2. The quality of our mental content can be continuously improved. In the mental storehouse of the individual much space is now occupied by facts or ideas which are relatively unimportant and inert. This 'wasted space' can be used for more significant facts or ideas as they are discovered or created.

3. The useful facts of the world do not have to be carried about in each and every mind. A division of intellectual labour is demonstrated by the high efficiency of a modern technological community in which a division of function exists among many experts and types of experts. Daily we push buttons whose operation is based upon facts we each individually need not comprehend. With the accumulation of new social know-

ledge, this process can doubtless go on to continuously higher levels of efficiency and safety.

From such considerations as the above it would seem more accurate to think of the potentialities of human intelligence not as finite but rather as indefinite, not to say unlimited. This hope for an endless increase in man's intellectual efficiency, however, rests most heavily upon our faith in human intelligence as the instrument for discovering new truths. Cancel this and reasonable hope for rapid progress disappears.

Much of the disparagement of human intelligence comes from its failure to solve problems where the necessary facts are not as yet revealed. Obviously, the cure is to be found in those arrangements which channel more of our intellectual energies into a search for the facts which are missing.

Many people are inclined to overlook this most obvious lack of necessary and relevant information because of the vast amount of information in the total pile of knowledge already acquired. There is a very widespread tendency to argue that we don't need more knowledge because we don't use the knowledge we now possess. Let us suggest that only relevant knowledge is usable. When we find the knowledge unused, we had better question its completeness or its relevancy. The inability of the human mind to make practical use of incomplete information is not a valid argument against our power to use adequate knowledge. It is an argument for using our intelligence to discover the essential and missing parts. Probably we shall find many of these most crucially missing facts in the realm of attitude. To know that disarmament is our need but not to know how to bring it about illustrates the tragedy of incomplete knowledge.

It has been well said that there is no substitute for intelligence. In the long run and from the broad perspective of the race as a whole, it seems inevitable that untold suffering and endless disappointment become the price we pay for our failure to use this biologically unique tool promptly in ways and places appropriate to our needs. On the other hand, there is no greater occasion for hope than to contemplate the degree to which human intelligence has compensated for other limitations of the human organism. Man has compensated for his physical limits—the length of his legs, the strength of his arms, the range of his voice. He has made up for the lack of thickness of his hide to protect himself from the weather; for the absence of wings to carry him over the seas and the mountains; for his absence of strength and speed to deliver him from attack of other animals. Man has used his intelligence to modify his physical environment and to adapt himself to it, and thereby has made himself the most physically comfortable and most powerful of all animals. Note that in all this he has discarded none of his capacities. He has used his brain in such ways as to extend vastly his sensory and muscular limits.

But there are other limits which need to be extended—spiritual, emotional, attitudinal limits. There are limits to man's courage, to his generosity, to his ability to co-operate. Why cannot these be compensated for by the appropriate use of his intelligence? We no longer believe in limits for the eventual speed of human travel. Why assume limits to human sympathy and co-operation?

Let us not stumble over the false notion that there is little relation between what we know or think and what we feel or want. Along with other creatures of the earth, man is a creature of needs and wants. But in contrast to other animals, he has an enormous capacity for the conscious development or clarification of his wants, as well as enormous resources for discovering reliable means for their satisfaction. Needs are not functional until they become wants. As wants, they become validly functional when they represent valid goals of satisfaction. In this process, intellect serves two functions; first, in advising what our needs are in their relation to the basic satisfaction implied by our nature and our circumstance. A new need discovered is a new knowledge come alive. Second, our intellect furnishes us the knowledge for implementing our wants. In brief, our intelligence helps both to improve and satisfy our wants. Men have long needed uncontaminated water. Recently many of us have come to want it pure and to understand how to get it purified.

However great the need for faith in the power of intelligence to reveal more and relevant facts, the amount of this faith is dangerously low on two counts. For one thing, we are always in danger of centring our eyes on the past. It is easier to be enthusiastic about what we have discovered than about what we need to discover. This is a great general handicap to crusades for new truth. In the second place this is particularly true in those areas where new truths are most needed. Naturally, our faith in human intelligence is greatest in those areas where our facts are most replete. In those areas where we have least succeeded in conquering our ignorance, we have the least support for believing in the efficacy of human inquiry. For sustaining our hope for more light in our darkest areas, we need the vision that enables us to make a transfer from satisfaction with progress achieved to confidence in progress yet to be achieved.

In order to remove unnecessary strain on our credulity, let us point out those excessive respects in which we do not have to have faith. As we have pointed out, we need not expect the intellectual worker to make bricks of understanding without the straws of information. Moreover, the faith discussed here is not a faith in the intellectual omnipotence of a single individual. We need not expect an infinite quality of intelligence to make up for a lack of quantity. If one or two or three individuals do not succeed in solving a problem, this is no evidence that the problem would not yield if attacked by a thousand or a million intellects.

Nor is an unbridled faith desirable. For the practical purpose of meeting timely emergencies, the total quantity of intelligence in the world is not unlimited. Misspent or misdirected intelligence cannot be expected to bring satisfactory results. To be concrete and realistic, we need to conceive intelligence in terms of man-hours and man-years. Any hour that is consumed by problem X cannot be devoted to problem Y. Students and workers in universities and other laboratories who spend their time in pursuit of those subjects and projects conducive to the increase of man's physical power cannot spend this same time in areas of study and research conducive to increasing man's social harmony. The race between catastrophe by war and peace by peaceful research is a function of relative time—the relative number of man-hours in which intelligence is applied to these different types of problems.

Tragic consequences may flow from the assumption that intelligence is entirely self-directable. The failure of intelligence in the past adequately to improve the lot of mankind can be attributed partly to a false faith that intelligence is beneficent regardless of the motive. However, before taking up the factor of the motive necessary for intellectual direction, let us give attention to the equally important problem of intellectual method.

Article 4. The Method—Faith in Science

Possession and use of a tool is not enough. The method of its use is extremely important. Faith in any instrument is inseparable from our faith in our ability to find out how to use it. This is true of human intelligence, the tool by which we achieve new knowledge and increased understanding.

In progressive circles, the improvability of method is taken for granted. Where method stagnates, progress disappears. Especially pertinent is this principle to those activities by which new facts are uncovered and a new truth is born. A very crucial part of the scientific process is frequently overlooked. We refer to that part of the process in which we invent, discover, or develop the method for making our discoveries. As Professor Whitehead has said, the greatest invention is the method of invention.

Explicit faith in science in any particular field includes faith in the power of intelligence to fashion methods appropriate to the discovery of new facts in that field. The breadth of our faith in science is in the number of fields or areas in which we believe more adequate fact-finding methods can be developed.

There is an inspiring challenge in the recent sharp upturn in the rate at which the human mind discovers highly significant knowledge. Study of the human records as developed by anthropologists and other historians impresses one with the following striking facts. There has been no change in basic human intelligence in more than one hundred thousand years. The human brain has no more basic capacity for invention or discovery today than it had a thousand centuries ago. That is, there has been in this stretch of time no improvement in the physiological or innate equipment of grey cells with which man does his thinking. Only within the past ten thousand years has there occurred any sharp improvement in human living as a result of the exercise of human intelligence. Only within the past two or three centuries has human intelligence been making the discoveries that have produced our marvellous modern technological efficiency.

It appears, then, that only recently and rather suddenly have men somehow come around to making a more efficient use of this attribute we call intelligence. It is not that men did not previously think and search and discover. But recently men have been thinking about how to think and discover. It seems that only yesterday did human intelligence fall into the practice of constructive self-criticism. Surely the possibilities of this new trend have scarcely begun to be realized.

Now that we have hit upon the fashion of using our intelligence to discover new and better methods of inquiry, why not trust ourselves to continue and expand and even re-direct this inspiring fashion? If the human mind is capable of inventing continually better methods for exploring and exposing the secrets of behaviour of planets and plants and neutrons, why not trust human intelligence with the task of inventing better methods for discovering facts about the social behaviour of man himself? Why did human intelligence operate for so many millennia with so little attention to its method of operation? It seems that men did not trust their intelligence this much or in this way. They seemed unable to realize the extent of this creative capacity of the human mind.

But this sort of tragic oversight is not limited to the past. Today many people seem totally unaware of and unimpressed by this opportunity. Some are aware of these possibilities in physical areas but not in the areas where lie our toughest social problems.

A certain futuristic confidence is essential for breaking ground in urgently needed new directions. These new directions require moral and financial support to enable us to pull on our new scientific seven-league boots before we have worn them long enough to prove their worth. When the suggestion is made that we organize for research for the elimination of war, the negative and rhetorical retort comes back, 'How can such research proceed? How could you go about it? Until you can present us with a plan of operation—an outline of the process and method that such research will follow, we refuse to believe that such research is possible'. The antidote for all such negativistic attitude is to read the record of the past and dare to extrapolate. In physical science, we have been able to fashion scientific method for discoveries which have resulted in the elimination of drudgery and the annihilation of time and space to an amazing degree. There must abide tremendous potential in the creative capacity of human intellect. In the development of new and better methods for finding out how to find out, it would seem correct to say that we have scarcely scratched the surface of our possibilities. These possibilities are waiting to be explored by men who can be freed to do so.

The requisite faith, of course, is a faith in what science can do in the future. The critical factor is in the difference between the science of the future and science of the past. There must be both similarities and significant differences between the sciences of human and physical relations. Belief in a science or sciences of human relations is difficult if not impossible if we make all science synonymous with chemistry or physics or botany or zoology or astronomy. Science must be thought of as much more than all of these put together. Even if we add present-day anthropology, sociology, psychology and economics, we still do not have the picture of science as it may evolve in another decade or another century. We must resist the temptation to limit science to the sum of past and present concrete scientific operations.

Of course scientific method invention of the future does not have to start from scratch. The usefulness of certain principles is already well demonstrated, such as experimentation, objectivity and quantification. Certainly these can be further exploited. In new and untried fields we will have to discover how and where to experiment, how to become more objective, how to quantify. Furthermore, why should anyone assume that all or even the best of the basic principles are already discovered? New principles should be discoverable even in physical sciences. The need as well as the eventual possibility of their discovery would appear to be as great or greater in the difficult field of human relations, involving as it does the as yet highly elusive factor of human attitude.

The great need is for a simple faith that whatever be the problem of method, it is soluble. This is why it often seems more appropriate to speak, not merely of scientific method, but of scientific attitude (scientific spirit) as well. In new realms, the latter is prerequisite to the former. This attitude is essential if we are to discover new ways to pry loose the old walls that hide the facts we need. Such faith has functioned in the past. Where cynics and super-realists said a solution was impossible, intellectual perseverance succeeded. For any successful effort to find the road to peace, men require the faith which refuses to take NO for an answer to the everlasting question of 'evil' in human relations. Our scientific experience has demonstrated that scientific method can become creative in realms new to science. How else could science have started in the first place? How else could we have added new sciences from time to time?

It is true that this faith is based on partial evidence. We have not fully demonstrated that we can devise plan and method suited to successful search for the information necessary for peace. We have, however, demonstrated our method-devising ability in connection with problems which once looked just as knotty as the problems which we now face. These demonstrations have bred the general hypothesis on which our scientific attitude is based. To nurture this faith further, we need to look at science not specifically but profoundly—not merely historically but prophetically. To prophesy for science, it is necessary to appreciate its dynamic, creative, evolutionary nature. How can one contemplate its miraculous record without reverence for its limitless possibilities?

By way of summary, let us emphasize three essential features of this fourth aspect of faith. First, this is not a faith that science will remain what it is and where it is. It is a faith that change is inevitable. Science appears to be the most evolutionary phenomenon we know. Second, this is not a faith in the kind of science that will continue to give us progress in the directions that we are now going by giving us merely more of the same kinds of new information. Science cannot save us if it develops only in those areas suited to more and more physical power. Faith in science implies the possibility of its being redirected into new channels.

Third, our faith dare not rest on the assumption that this redirection will take place by the principle of scientific *laissez-faire*. In a certain sense, science is incapable of its own redirection. It will not develop in those areas where there is not sufficient provision for and encouragement of scientific workers. Science is not a magic entity that can work without human instrumentation. It grows in those areas where there are scientists at work. Human intelligence cannot find the secret of harmony and of peace and of survival if the major portion of our most serious and systematic intellectual effort continues to take place in the areas of physical relations and in the directions of more increase in mere physical power. A prime condition for the reasonableness of our faith is that intellectual energy become channelled into the area of human relations and dedicated to the progressive solution of the problem of human conflict.

This means that we cannot rest content to leave the scientific enterprise under the direction of those motives which now chiefly control it. Is there potentially adequate motivation for the redirection of the intellectual energies of mankind?

ARTICLE 5. THE MOTIVE—FAITH IN DEMOCRATIC OR HUMANISTIC MOTIVATION FOR SCIENCE

Indispensable to a science of global harmony is the *motive* of global welfare. Faith in a science of peace must include the faith that the scientific enterprise can be guided by the criterion of the greatest good for the greatest number. This includes the assumption of course that science can be humanistically motivated and still be science.

The motivational pattern of the past has been sufficient to develop a dynamic scientific movement and to achieve greater knowledge for power. It has not been adequate to guide the scientific movement to greater knowledge suitable for greater harmony.

To get at the problem of misorder in science, it is necessary to scrutinize the incentives by which the scientific enterprise is guided. How has science been motivated? Recognized by all observers of scientific effort is the motive of pure science or knowledge for knowledge's sake. Einstein, for instance, has said that his scientific activity has been motivated 'by an irresistible longing to understand the secrets of nature'. Sheer curiosity, however, is not the whole of scientific motivation. To a greater or lesser degree, sooner or later, some form of utilitarian incentive makes itself evident. Pasteur, for instance, seems to have been driven by a vision of a vast contribution of science to human welfare.

Today utilitarian motives are increasingly playing the major role, not only in industrial laboratories, but in our universities where huge subsidies are granted by agencies with special utilitarian interests. A high percentage of all present scientific research is now subsidized in the interest of industrial development or military defence. This springs primarily from the motive of commercial and national advancement. Speaking generally, we can label this the motive of partisan advantage. This is natural in a world of economic and inter-nation competition. Furthermore, such motive in our present setting naturally directs research toward more and more power. The theme song grows louder and louder—*Let us make our nation strong*.

Scientific statesmanship requires a broader and more generous viewpoint. Science is more and more a huge social enterprise. If you please, it is big business. It is serious business. It is, in terms of its vital consequences, the business of all people. For emphasis, let us say, *all peoples*. As this business goes well or ill, its blessing or blight will extend to all members of the human race everywhere. Now if this be true, it must be readily recognized that partisan motivation is inadequate and that wholeistic motivation is essential.

The crying need is for depth and breadth in the utilitarian part of the motivation. The motive needed is one which will cause concern, not only with matter, but with man and his attitudes. It must be broad enough to direct inquiry into the welfare of mankind as a whole. Scientific motivation need not be partial and partisan. It can be comprehensive and wholeistic. It must be so if we are to achieve world-wide harmony and survival.

The most crucial part of the scientific operation is scientific planning. This can be done safely and adequately today only by the type of individual who achieves an appreciable degree of identification between self and society as a whole. There is needed not only social motivation but motivation on the broadest democratic base. Our need is for scientific planning pitched at the planetary level. Of course, as with other matters, science will continue to be propelled by a mixture of motives. In this mixture, however, the most crucially needed element at present is this identification with and sympathy for all men regardless of creed or colour or race or nation.

But is there enough of this broad kind of democratic goodwill in the human animal? Can we afford to count on it?

Faith in a science of peace requires an affirmative answer. Faith for practical action must run somewhat as follows. We believe that a great many people—literally millions—are consciously desirous of seeing human frustration and suffering mitigated, not only within their own family, local community or nation, but throughout the whole human family. We believe there are a great many people whose sense of human interdependence is wider than that of colour or sect or nation or continent. There must be literally millions of people who have a restless realization that their personal welfare is dependent upon the welfare of our total world society.

Both the motive of human betterment and our faith in this motive can profit from a principle which is operative throughout nature—the principle of induction. This is the principle that, with dynamic material, a little can be used to induce more and result in much. This is true in bacteriology. This principle can work on the side of health and survival as well as of disease and destruction. However small and weak the motive for humanistic science, or however inexplicit the faith in this motive, there are always possibilities for development.

The principle that action leads to reaction can operate in our favour providing we can achieve the necessary initial expression. In the realm of human motivation, this feature of expression and response is all-important. Acts of altruism and humanism often stimulate acts of altruism and humanism by those in whom this quality otherwise lies dormant. Essential to human interaction is the fact of communication which requires expression of attitude (motive, faith, etc.). Here, as elsewhere, successful expression produces further expression.

Our faith, then, is not only that there is an appreciable amount of the motive of planetary democracy—broad humanitarianism—that it can be released and made operative, but that as we do so it will rapidly expand.

Just a word as to what this faith is not. It is not a faith in spiritual *laissez-faire*. This is not a faith that global patriotism, like murder, will out. Certain things come out only if we help them out. First of all, there is the principle of organization—getting together such people in such ways as are appropriate to the furtherance of the means and ends we have discussed. All the uranium in the world produced no chain reaction until somebody started the process of appropriate assemblage. All the goodwill in the world will remain impotent if not adequately organized. If there be no organization, there will be no chain reaction either among atoms or attitudes. Futhermore, in the realm of social relations, there can be no organization without a minimal amount of initial communication which in turn requires adequate expression on the part of the individual person.

With regard to the faith which we are here discussing, justification for more faith comes with any added evidence that others have it. Here, if anywhere, we have illustration that a shared asset is an increased asset.

This then is the answer to the conditions required for a sustained faith in the humanitarian motive of man. It requires expression. The writing of this book is one such expression. The reaction of the reader is another and more important expression.

Summary

In the past chapters we have said that, for survival and progress, our society needs peace and harmony. Peace and harmony require scientific research. Particularly and pointedly we need now a science of peace. In this chapter we have stressed that to get a science of peace under way requires a new faith. Faith in a science of peace can be achieved by combining and emphasizing separate faiths. These we already have, but they require interlocking for mutual or reciprocal support. We started with faith in the achievability of human harmony, to be made possible by pertinent and new knowledge. Faith in the discoverability of such knowledge is conditioned by our faith in human intelligence and our faith in science or the improvability of intellectual method. All this is conditioned by our faith in democratic motivation to channel properly our intellectual energy and to redirect our scientific enterprise in ways that will yield the necessary knowledge. These separate elements of our faith can no longer logically thrive separately and apart from each other. They must combine.

More briefly stated, survival requires a functional unity of our faith in science and our faith in democracy. The scientific attitude and the democratic attitude are not suitable for use on separate days and for separate occasions. Essential to survival is the faith that the 'all-powerful method of science' can be invoked in behalf of our democratic idealism. The need is for the faith which fuses in the same act our positive and active reverence for life with an uninhibited passion for truth. Scientific man is already here. He yet needs to be democratized. Democracy's charm is recognized by many people in many places. The ideal has yet to be made real. For this, scientific intelligence is required. Let us think of a science of peace as part of the science of culture. Faith in such science can be part of our faith in the endless improvability of man.

This total pattern of belief presented in these five articles is to be considered more or less tentative and testable. No aspect of it should be considered as rigidly fixed or final. For misstatements and omissions, we stand correctible. Our faith in the power of new knowledge to increase our understanding and efficiency implies the expectation of continuous and progressive change in our point of view. Improvement necessitates change. Change for the better requires the detection of weaknesses and errors not only in technique of research, but also in basic assumptions on which the research action is to be founded.

But what about alternative approaches to peace? In advocating a science of peace, we have not said that other proposals for peace action are necessarily invalid. Our central theme is that we need to search for the road to peace. To say that our need is for peace know-how is not to say that all present and previous proposals are completely invalid. What is needed is neither wholesale rejection nor blanket acceptance. What is needed is over-all and critical and specific inspection.

Our contention is merely that our first, wisest, next action is research action. We need enough scepticism or open-mindedness to insist upon testing our current convictions and upon experimenting with new conceptions. However much anyone may believe in the effectiveness of any particular peace programme, he should expect it to profit by careful scientific study. It would seem that any believer in any programme would welcome increased efficiency of action. If, for instance, we are to be saved by some approach through religion, education, or economics, it will have to be an improved religious or educational or economic approach.

These improvements can come best if we come at them intelligently, experimentally, and objectively. To illustrate, let us consider such an obvious eventual necessity as disarmament. Scientific peace workers would spend their energy neither in arguing for nor against this proposal. They would ask, first: Is disarmament conducive to peace? second: Under what circumstances? third: Can it be brought about? and fourth: By what procedure? Any other proposal would receive similar consideration to determine its plausible, possible appropriateness in the minds of those whose high concern is the *Know-how for Peace*.

Now one more repetition. If survival depends upon peace, if peace depends upon peace know-how, if the know-how depends upon peace research, and if peace research depends upon our faith in peace research—upon what does this faith depend?

It depends, above all else, upon intercommunication among those who possess enough of it to say so. The great danger is that those who believe will not recognize one another. The great need is for the believers to pool their moral and intellectual and financial resources. He who has discovered his faith in the scientific search for peace must find other believers. Contact with others of like faith is indispensable on two counts. First, morale is vital. Awareness of and confidence in others of similar intention is essential to one's courage. Second, war elimination is a co-operative job. Co-operation is never possible without consciousness of common purpose.

Man is peculiarly equipped as a signalling or communicating animal. Let him use this signal equipment freely. Let each one who knows that he believes in a science of peace make it known. Let consciousness of common goal develop. Let there be mutual recognition among those who share consciousness of our common ignorance. Along with the spirit of the Chinese proverb: Curse not the darkness; light a candle.

7
WHAT IS MEANT BY A SCIENCE OF PEACE?

IN this chapter, we want to point out those respects in which science, as a method, is basically suited to peace as a problem. We trust that this will give some sort of impression of what the process will be like when the problem and the method are mated. Let us emphasize first some of the characteristics of science as it has thus far operated. This is our best response to those who ask for a definition of science. No one of these characteristics taken alone completely differentiates science from non-science.

In Chapter 5 we pointed out that, with peace as with other problems, the solution waits for the discovery of new and relevant knowledge. But how does the scientific discovery of new knowledge take place? Briefly stated, it occurs through the intense use of intelligence to formulate questions and pursue their answers through systematic observation and careful consideration leading to inference which can be objectively tested. The choice of questions is controlled by rigorous regard for their relevance to a particular problem. We will add to this our insistent proposal that the choice of the problem be controlled with relevance to the goal of over-all human betterment and with democratic regard for the common wishes of mankind. This will require modification of scientific ethics, but need not violate any essential scientific principle.

A science of peace might include *the intensive and systematic study of any matters that seem relevant to war and peace.* These will be primarily, or at least initially, matters of human feeling and understanding and interaction, but anything relevant is in order. There should be no limit placed upon the range of operation of the science of peace except the limit of relevance. If wars are caused by glands or sunspots, let us find out. The determination of what matters are most likely relevant will be progressive, changing from stage to stage in the development of the science.

Science as Intelligence

P. W. Bridgman has defined science as 'the free and utmost use of intelligence'. This is not explicitly inclusive but calls attention to one of the most crucial factors. From this point of view, one might define a science of peace as an enterprise where a considerable number of interested men are free to put forth their utmost of collective intellectual effort to discover the know-how for peace.

We too often are prone to look at the external feature of science and mistake the incidental for the essential. The layman thinks of test tubes and Bunsen burners as that which makes a science. He is less likely to picture the mind within which burns the flame of curiosity without which the scientific enterprise could not go on. Even the scientist himself, being so close to the trees, may miss the essential outlines of the forest. It is the purpose of this inquiry to attempt to reach and explain the most basic factors involved in the scientific enterprise. Let us therefore keep always in mind this first generalization that science is intelligence operating at its most intense and efficient level. The test tubes are incidental.

Surely peace is a problem which we should attack with the greatest intellectual resources at our command. We should attack it inquiringly, imaginatively, realistically, and with all the relevance our intellect can design, and with all the democracy we can muster.

If it be within the capacity of human intelligence to solve the problem of war, and yet we fail to make the investment, that will be the greatest tragedy of all time. To fail to invest our intellectual capital first and most in our foremost problem is neither ethical nor intelligent. This becomes especially poignant when we contemplate the vast quantities of intelligence now being invested in problems or activities universally admitted to be of much less importance. The investment of intelligence in competitive armament at such a terrific rate alongside such a meagre investment of intelligence in the direction of co-operative politics implies that we humans have been caught in a culture immorally indiscriminate regarding the investment of intelligence.

We expend tremendous amounts of intelligent effort on relatively trivial distinctions among brands of automobiles, chewing-gum, or liquor. Surely we can afford to put equal or greater intellectual effort into the distinction between those practices

WHAT IS MEANT BY A SCIENCE OF PEACE?

which debase and threaten to extinguish and those which can promise to continue and expand and refine our civilization. One of our greatest co-operative opportunities is in co-operation at the level of high intelligence.

But just how does intelligence at the scientific level differ from intelligence at levels pre-scientific or non-scientific? The first feature that impresses the author is that of the quantity of intelligence concentrated upon a given problem. If our intelligence has not solved a problem, then one possible remedy is to apply more of it. The greater the problem the individual faces, the more of the individual's attention is called for. The greater the problem, the greater the number of individuals required to solve it. (This necessity for quantity does not imply absence of necessity for quality).

That an individual or a group of individuals must give sufficient time and intelligence to a problem if they hope to solve it, is a matter of elementary logic. But then there arises a very common experience. Each individual is confronted with so many problems. There is a solution for this, common not only to science but to civilization in general. It is to apply the principle of division of labour. Although, if an individual isn't a match for 100 problems 10,000 individuals might easily solve these 100 problems if, and only if, the individuals divide up the problems. Schematically speaking, it thus becomes possible for the individuals to outnumber their problems, 100 to one.

This possibility of a division of labour by which men can solve one another's scientific problems is due to the repetitive factor in nature. Certain type problems occur over and over. A number of problems of a great many people throughout the world are similar. When human intelligence develops solutions for problems or partial solutions or partial knowledge looking toward solutions, in such a way that it is transferable from one mind to another, then we have science. Any research or any thinking that an individual does, which he cannot eventually transfer to other individuals or other thinkers, hardly meets the criterion of science.

Asking Questions

One of the most simple and fundamental views of science is to view it as an inquiring or questioning enterprise. The disposition for asking questions plays a heavy role in making man intelligent.

In large measure, intelligence functions by way of the mechanism of asking questions and searching for answers.

Questioning gets on, in part at least, by means of a very common and elementary behaviour tendency—curiosity. Here we have a trait which is inseparable from man's progress. By the instrumentation of the question mark, man has invited himself out of the jungle on to the highways of civilization. He has asked himself out of the primitive cold and dark and wet and, most important of all, out of his intellectual darkness.

Curiosity points always in the direction of the new and the the unknown. It is the urge which causes facts to shift from the realm of the unknown to the known. It operates as a hunger—a hunger for information or knowledge or understanding. Curiosity is an attitude. In referring to it as an attitude, we must not forget that, like all attitudes, it can be a dynamic developing process. It varies from person to person. Within the same person, it varies from time to time and from object to object. This variation is our challenge. Curiosity can be cultivated. A science of peace requires conditions favourable for cultivating intense and unrelenting curiosity about the cause and cure of war. These conditions, of course, should not be left to chance.

Curiosity requires guidance. Judging by our progress, we have asked a great many effective questions. Some of our questions surely have been the right questions. However, considering the present threat to our survival, we have occasion to reflect upon the incompleteness of our questioning. Some crucial questions seem to have been omitted thus far. We seem to be proving our capacity to be curious about the right things in the wrong order. Let us beware lest the proverb 'curiosity killed a cat' come to mean 'curiosity killed a race'.

We would like to call attention to a high degree of sameness in the meaning of the two words, *problem* and *question*. To have no questions about a situation means that we do not recognize it as a problem. Any problem we can recognize, we can ask questions about. Anywhere we can ask sensible questions, we can, granted time and intelligence, develop a science. In brief, any problem that is recognizable is subject to scientific attack. Too many don't recognize peace as a problem. They seem to assume that they 'know the answers'.

Of course a great many people have already asked questions

WHAT IS MEANT BY A SCIENCE OF PEACE?

about peace and war, but there is a difference between the non-scientific and the scientific type of question. The challenge of this book is that we get set to pay the price for trading off our pre-scientific or non-scientific questions about peace for those that are scientific. This is indispensable if we want the problem of peace solved.

Characteristic of the scientific type of questioning is the greater degree of seriousness with which the scientist takes his questions. ' "What is truth?" said jesting Pilate: and would not stay for an answer.' Seriousness leads to persistence. Persistence leads to absorption and concentration and specialization. This results in a high degree of expertness or skill. The scientist cannot attend to a thousand and one subjects in one day or even one lifetime. The scope and depth, the quantity and quality of questions a person or group of persons can ask about a specific problem, depends upon the amount of intelligence which has been concentrated on the problem and within the area in which it develops. The expert in a given area will likely be more creative in formulating questions and be a better judge of a relevant question when he sees one.

Scientific from non-scientific activity can be distinguished by the emphasis placed upon the formulation of the question. Albert Einstein says:

> Galileo formulated the problem of determining the velocity of light, but did not solve it The formulation of a problem is often more essential than its solution, which may be merely a matter of mathematical or experimental skill. To raise new questions, new possibilities, to regard old problems from a new angle, requires creative imagination and marks real advance in science.

An important criterion of successful formulation of a question is answerability. Is the question susceptible of being answered in its present form? If not, it is said not to be an *operational* question and must be reframed or traded off for a question for which there is hope of an answer. A question is proved operational as one succeeds in desiging an operation which can contribute to its answer. This involves trial and error by thinkers of imagination and perseverance. The goal is meaningful questions meaningfully answered.

THE QUESTION PROCESS

The search for truth operates by way of a continuity of successive questions and answers. In this question process, the questioner and his questions undergo a progressive change and his answers mount up to a pile increasingly satisfying and provocative to further and more profound questions. The investigator's insight progresses. His questions penetrate further. His answers accumulate toward a point or points where they first enable the scientist to understand and predict, and then the technician or the layman to control events. The scientist discovers the effects of certain drugs upon sensitivity to pain. The technician produces the aspirin tablet. The layman with a headache swallows it.

Scientific research can be thought of as somewhat resembling the process in a dialogue, in the sense that interaction takes place between the question or stimulus and the answer or response. If the response is silence (no answer), the questioner may repeat his question, but sooner or later, if persistent, he will either obtain a satisfying answer or change the form of his question. The difference between a non-scientifically and a scientifically curious person may be seen in the extent to which frustration on the one hand deadens and on the other sharpens curiosity.

The question process is also a process of question change in terms of shift from higher to lower levels of observation. With regard to peace, we might refer to the highest level as represented by the question, 'How can we get peace?' This question can be divided into such further questions as, 'Can we get peace by preparing for war?' Or, 'Is the cure for war to be found in formal education?' A sub-division of this latter question might be, 'Do college graduates on the average have a different attitude toward war or matters related thereto than do people with merely high-school education?'

In obtaining the answer to this question, it might be necessary to ask many college and high-school graduates specific questions bearing upon attitudes which appear to be relevant to peace and war. The college and the non-college person might be asked, 'Do you favour World Government?' Suppose we refer to this last type of question as the number-three-level question and the original question, 'How can we get peace?' as a number-one-level question. Let all the others in between represent the number-two-level questions.

Suppose further we conceive of the number-three-level questions as furnishing answers to specific number-two-level questions, and answers to the number-two-level questions as being necessary

WHAT IS MEANT BY A SCIENCE OF PEACE?

to get the answer to the number-one-level question. The research process then is one of dividing and sub-dividing the questions until we get a question which is directly answerable by observation or interview. The answers then to questions at one level need to be added or combined to produce the answer to a higher-level question. That is, several thousand questions at the number three level may be necessary to answer one question at the number two level, and answers to a good many number-two-level questions are necessary for the number-one-level answer.

Now this scientific question process of dividing or analysing the questions plus the reverse process of adding or combining the answers carries with it the possibility of division of labour, previously mentioned. The possibility of combining the answers is vitally essential to the division of labour in the scientific enterprise. Unless we can divide the work, and unless we can summate the answers, no large-scale co-operative truth-seeking enterprise is practical. Our scientific literature in physical science is full of illustrations of this co-ordination and co-operation involving the division of labour and the cumulative effect of the findings of thousands of separate and more or less independent investigators.

Division of labour is essential to speed and acceleration in the development of a science. Division of questions and division of labour make possible and usable an enormous increase in the number of investigators. Physics and chemistry are accelerating in their findings and resultant potency, at the present moment, but it must not be forgotten that there is a terrific acceleration in the growth in sheer numbers of physicists and chemists. This acceleration involving multitudes of scientists is further made possible by the power of scientists to communicate with one another. The language of science is built up in the interest of effective and economical inter-communication.

SCIENTIFIC VERSUS NON-SCIENTIFIC ANSWERS

As with the form of the question, so with the answers to the question, scientific inquiry sets a higher standard than ordinary question-asking. Answers that seem to satisfy the inexpert often prove to be on closer inspection no answers at all. To the question, 'What causes war?' the answer, 'Human greed' cannot long satisfy the skilled and serious interrogator. This answer gives no basis for control either over war or over greed. One important criterion of a scientific answer is: Does the answer contribute to the eventual answering of other and higher-level questions?

As of 1954 the human race is the possessor (in the persons of its experts) of a large block of information which constitutes what is called a science of bacteriology. Included in this factual structure is the answer of Pasteur and others, namely, 'microbes', to the question, 'What causes epidemic sickness?' To the question, 'Do mosquitoes and mosquito bites cause yellow fever?' there were numerous 'yes' or 'no' answers, but Walter Reed's standard for an answer to this question was relatively high and could not be satisfied in his opinion, short of an expensive and dangerous experiment. With such carefully controlled answers the science of bacteriology has been able to progress to the point of the saving of millions of lives.

One feature that characterizes scientific search for answers is the great care in the observing of that which is being studied. Somewhere in the expenditure of scientific energy comes a sizeable item for gathering data—for making direct and immediate observations with the five senses. The scientist requires relatively more direct overt experience with the content of life than does the casual questioner. The observations of yesterday are not enough. We must continue to look and to listen, to smell and to taste and to feel, as well as to think.

Since the scientist is interested in adequate answers to important questions, he is more likely in his persistence to take time to develop tools for his process. Thus scientific questions include tool questions. How can we observe better? In response to this we have a great array of instruments from telescopes to microscopes for increasing the range and acuity of the human sense organs. A successful science of peace will have to place due emphasis upon better techniques for gathering the relevant raw facts involved.

We must continue our measurements, say the scientists. We cannot afford to neglect either observation or interpretation—sensation or cerebration. Tremendous amounts of high intelligence have been wasted because of unwillingness to pay the price for additional data.

Now one clue to the fact of fallacy in an answer is that of disagreement among the answers of different observers and interpreters. One of the key words in science is that of objectivity.

WHAT IS MEANT BY A SCIENCE OF PEACE?

The touchstone for objectivity is the degree of agreement from observer to observer when all the observers are focusing upon the same object. When the observation varies from observer to observer, we say that the process is subjective; i.e., it is a function of the observer and not of the object being observed. The generalized formula in cases of disagreement among observers is that of re-inspection or re-observation, or retrial when the observation is associated with some sort of manipulative experimentation. If an international event or situation is observed or interpreted contradictorily by individuals on opposite sides of an international boundary line, we must not accept this conflict of evidence as insoluble. We must increase the number of observers and observational viewpoints. This must not be done on the level of diplomacy or of propaganda, but in the spirit of honest scientific inquiry.

In certain areas of human curiosity such as astronomy, we take it for granted that if there is a disagreement about the movement of planets or other bodies, time will be found, somewhere, somehow, by someone to make the necessary additional observations. In the realm of human relations, however, we are only beginning to build up devotion to this method of solution. If men disagree as to the role of big business in provoking us into war, the decision too often is left to the skill of emotionalized dialectic. The resort to additional facts as practised in physics, chemistry, botany, zoology is somehow too often and too much missing.

When is a fact a fact? In science one very important criterion is that of prediction. Do these facts enable us to make verifiable predictions as to what will happen under carefully specified conditions? Increased ability to predict events is one of the greatest contributions which science has made to human respect for human intelligence. Let us give one illustration. Astronomers have predicted that at a specified hour of a specified day of a specified year in the twenty-first century people in Paris will (if any exist) witness an eclipse of the sun. No one expects the prediction to miss by more than a few seconds. This prediction and confidence in it are based upon previous study and verified regularity of movement of heavenly bodies in the past few centuries. In a very broad sense some form of prediction is found in all scientific fields. It is most striking in fields of experimental science. This kind of verification or evidence brings agreement from the most sceptical. This growth in man's power of prediction is bought at the expense of myriads of hours of careful observation and patient and profound reflection. We say these predictions are based on law—on long-standing but recently discovered laws (regularities in cause and effect of events).

Frequently the history of these discoveries has indicated that they are first sensed in a very broad way and much later refined by careful study of qualifying conditions. This might well become increasingly true in research on human relations. In the past few decades many of us have been amazed at the startling success of the Gandhian Movement of non-violent resistance in India. It has been greeted with both admiration and scepticism. Will it harmonize the world? Can it be counted on to extend human freedom? Under what conditions? Will it work in South Africa? In the Eastern Zone of Germany? Will it produce racial equality in the United States? Can we specify the kind of master that will turn out to be amenable to this kind of resistance? And the kind of 'slave' who can resist non-violently?

Recently a scientist working at the Hoover Institute at Stanford, California (U.S.A.) developed a new phrase to represent an old concept. This phrase is 'reciprocity of attitude'. If X loves and trusts Y, Y will love and trust X. If nation X fears and arms against nation Y, nation Y will reciprocate. Heretofore we have heard a good deal (idealistically) about reciprocity as an 'ought' and relatively little (realistically) about it as an 'is'. How often *is* it a fact? It seems that here is a golden opportunity for the history of scientific man to repeat itself. Why not a few million man hours of study of the conditions under which attitudinal reciprocity does and does not take place?

The Factor of Relevance

Let us now make explicit a very critical characteristic of behaviour among scientists which was implied in what has already been said about the question and answer process. This is their rigorous regard for the principle of relevance. In contrast to the non-scientific, scientific observation might be designated as observation with a purpose. The purpose is to find the answer to a given question. All answers to a low-level question are relevant to answering a specified question at the next higher level, and so

WHAT IS MEANT BY A SCIENCE OF PEACE?

on up the scale. This strict intellectual and research discipline is inseparable from the scientific method and its amazing success. However, the scientists' regard for relevance is far from perfect.

Both the value of this principle and our shortcomings in applying it at the higher levels can be made clearer by the following simplified illustration. Suppose your reporter came upon a scientist in charge of a large research staff devoted to the goal of atomic bombs. Let us invision the following dialogue.

> Reporter: 'Why are you carrying on these experiments?'
> Scientist: 'To find out how to get plutonium from uranium 238.'
> Reporter: 'Why do you want to find out how to get plutonium from uranium 238?'
> Scientist: 'Because we want to find out how to make cheaper and more plentiful and more powerful bombs.'
> Reporter: 'Why do we need to find out about a more plentiful supply of more powerful bombs?'
> Scientist: 'In order to answer a further question.'
> Reporter: 'And what is that?'
> Scientist: 'How can we increase our security.'
> Reporter: (With justifiable scepticism) 'Do more and more bombs, with more and more power, increase our security?'
> Scientist: 'This question has not been assigned to our department.'

Here the reporter and the scientist might agree that if an open-minded approach be made to the question of how best to increase our security, the question of how to produce more effective bombs might not appear to be highly relevant.

The tragedy of the scientific enterprise and of the whole enterprise of civilization may come because of our failure to respect adequately the principle of relevance at these higher levels. The proposal for a science of peace is a proposal to direct our intelligence to and develop our interrogativity to the major question, 'How can we survive?' 'What can we do to save our civilization from its presently threatened disruption?' The pragmatic test of which modern science is said to be the offspring must be applied to science itself. Does science really and finally work? Does it eventually produce what is wanted by human beings? Does it add up to all that we have a right to expect?

We are here faced with one of the great dangers of division of labour. In science as elsewhere there is the possibility of dangerous omissions. A family in which no one chooses to look after food might starve. A city in which no one chooses to look after health might suffer epidemic disaster. An atomic age global society in which no one chooses to look after peace may become extinct.

Using science for certain ends such as national and partisan security has got the scientific minds of men on to wrong tracks. *Re*-orientation and *Re*-direction are imperative. Science needs, for instance, to devise better avenues of approach to the problem of security than are found in those researches which foster the armament race. We need to ask regarding our questions, not only is the question relevant to the problem, but is the problem relevant to our universal safety and hence to the eventual solution of our various problems? As questions need to be designed to fit into a larger well-designed set of questions to make an integrated science, so sciences need to be designed to fit into a set of sciences to make an integrated culture. Having failed to do this, we now find ourselves in a dizzily evolving culture faced with possible if not probable disintegration. Part of the secret of an integrated culture is in an integrated science, or set of sciences. Our proposal is that investment in a science of peace, as a part of a science of culture, is a prime approach to this problem. Whatever the problem of integration may require in the future, a science of peace appears now to be highly relevant and essential to survival.

Democratization of Science

If we are correct in suggesting that science has operated first in the wrong place, how shall we cure this? How shall this need for higher relevance be achieved? We propose the formula *the democratization of science*. Somehow we will have to get science and scientific direction to be sensitive to the common will of common people. We know that curiosity is not the only desirable attitudinal trait. Man, who wants to know, wants more than to know. The question which the spectacle of science presents to the human mind at the present moment runs something like this: 'Does more physical power represent our greatest desire?' 'Do we most want faster planes, greater comforts of shelter, greater ease in the production of food and clothing?' 'Would we the people of the world rather have science devoted to greater weapons or greater peace?' If there is no agency or set of specialists adequately set up and experienced for determining the will of the people on these and other points, such an agency and experience can be developed.

In a highly democratized science who is to take responsibility for putting the questions at the various levels? Let the technicians in social science put the questions at the third level. The more highly skilled scientific thinkers are required for effective formulation of questions at the second or middle level. At the highest level it is our contention that the question belongs to the people, who have a stake in the question, and who are at the mercy of our ignorance involved in the question. In the case of the number one question, 'How get rid of war?' this involves the whole human race. It should not be left to any small segment of society to decide whether this question deserves to be answered.

If we are disturbed that scientists have been taking orders from partisan or competitive persons or interests, let us bestir ourselves. We propose, for instance, that it is within the capacity of common men to decide whether they want to subsidize scientific research on the number-one-level question of how some nations can win wars, or whether they want to subsidize scientific research on the question of how to eliminate wars. Our general contention is that the democratization of science is fully as important as the democratization of any other part of the human enterprise. This means that science be both *for* and *by* the people. This is especially true of a science *of* people. The people must have something to say about where the scientific method is to be applied. There are levels of operation of the scientific process which are too complicated for those of us who are not specialists. But there is no reason why we, the people of the world, should not have scientific research done through our agents—agents who act in line with our highest need and our deepest wish.

Summary

In this chapter we have discussed the possibility of putting together an outstanding question or problem and an outstanding method and fact. The question or problem is, 'How can we get peace?' The outstanding method is that of science. The outstanding fact is the efficacy of this method for solving problems.

Regarding the method, we have emphasized the idea that there is nothing peculiar in the nature of science. All men use intelligence. Science results where intelligence is more appropriately directed and more highly focused. Intelligence in general and scientific intelligence in particular operate through the question process. All men ask questions. Scientists ask questions in a more systematic and rigorous fashion. Science has grown as men have insisted that our various questions with their answers should have a certain relatedness or relevance to one another.

We have suggested that the nature of the problem of peace is such that we can ask answerable questions about it that are relevant to it. The greatest block to a science of peace is the lack of a clear recognition of peace as a problem. Our greatest need is a clear recognition that peace represents something that we desire but do not know how to get. Questions about war and peace can be made answerable through the process of creative imagination coupled with observation since war and peace are matters of human behaviour. Human behaviour is observable, providing we have the confidence to take the pains to see it. We have suggested that questions are divisible and relatable and that answers thereto are not only obtainable but combinable.

We have suggested that an essential principle in all this is that of relevance and that our failure to survive would be due to our failure to continue the process of relating our questions and adding our answers up to include the number-one-level question of how can we get peace and harmony. We have suggested that a safe and needed criterion of the proper number one or over-all controlling question of science is the criterion of what the people need and potentially want to have discovered—want to know—all the people. Bringing the scientific enterprise under democratic control will not be easy but enormously worth-while. 'The marriage of sanctity and science' has been suggested but not consummated.

The question is not, 'Can scientific method save us?' or 'Could it?' Rather the question is, 'Will we develop and use it? Do we have the courage, the confidence, the morale to use our intelligence relevantly and co-operatively?' In the following chapter we wish to illustrate that broad and comprehensive planning of research on human understandings and misunderstandings relevant to peace is possible.

8
OUTLINING THE RESEARCH

CAN a comprehensive programme of research be designed? This chapter is presented to illustrate that the practical planning of a science of peace is possible. This illustration should, of course, be taken as minimal evidence. Granted greater resources of time and intelligence, something much deeper and broader would surely become quickly realized. The final plan may turn out to be much simpler than the picture here presented. However, neither the difficulty of the task of planning, nor the importance of good planning must be minimized. Since this chapter is somewhat more technical than the others some readers may prefer to skip it, partly or wholly.

WHAT KIND OF QUESTIONS?

In Chapters 1 and 2 we emphasized the obvious fact that wars are caused by people. Our basic platform for this chapter includes the assumption that better understanding of people by people is essential for peace. Therefore the research task is to bring about this greater understanding. A profound but highly simplified statement in this connection is found in the first sentence of the charter of U N E S C O. 'Since wars are made in the minds of men, it is in the minds of men that the foundations of peace must be constructed.' This need not be taken as a contradiction to other statements such as 'Wars are made in men's stomachs' or 'Wars are made in or by our institutions' or 'by our diplomats'. Hunger does influence man's reaction, mental and otherwise, but an empty stomach does not always lead to war and a full stomach does not always lead to peace. As pointed out in Chapter 3 we are the victims of a bad pattern of institutions. But institutions are maintained by men on the basis of what men rightly or wrongly believe they can get out of them. Diplomats do have a role to play in preventing war. But diplomats are people. Moreover there are other people who influence them. All these people have minds.

Let us repeat this general idea using the concept of *belief*. Whether war and war preparation are continued or discontinued depends upon what peoples and nations *believe* about one another. We stand to gain immeasurably by detailed verification or correction of this hypothesis. Surely the research can be so conducted as to reveal any total or partial fallacy in this assumption. Other plans for research can of course be projected from other viewpoints. Proceeding on the one we have here started, our goal becomes clear, viz., to uncover the fiction and the reality in 'the picture in our heads' about one another (and ourselves[1]). One antidote to false belief is fact. The remedy for misunderstanding is understanding. The antidote to error and mutual suspicion is truth and mutual trust.

At this stage let us use the term 'mind' broadly. War and peace are matters of inter-nation interaction. Human interaction is never purely a function of what we know. It is determined also by how we feel. The word 'mind' must be here understood to cover more than intelligence. It must include attitude. Our perpetual inquiry needs to be, 'How do the nations feel towards one another and on what do these feelings rest?'

Size and Scope

The sheer number of questions eventually to be answered will probably prove to be enormous. Several million more or less minor questions had to be answered to answer the major question: How can an explodable uranium bomb be developed? Comparably for the question: 'How can democratic global unity be achieved?' we will doubtless need to answer millions of minor questions in political psychology and other fields. Of course the number of questions, minor and specific, that need to be answered for an adequate and functional science of peace cannot now be accurately predicted. However, we had better not underestimate their number.

Included among our questions will be not only questions which are relevant, essential and answerable. Included also will be questions which initially seem to be relevant, but which will eventually be shown to be unessential and, in the last analysis, irrelevant and

---

[1] As Alexander Leighton has said 'If "Know thyself" is a good rule for individual men, it is a good rule for nations also'. Most probably self understanding comes best in an objective perspective where the self is included in the larger setting of all peoples or nations.

perhaps foolish. The inclusion of this latter group in our working operation arises out of one simple inescapable fact—namely, the inability of the scientist to predict perfectly which questions are going to prove happy and pertinent leads to the necessary and relevant fact. If a sincere and intelligent scientific worker be observed by a critical observer to be concerning himself with foolish question number 37,377, he should not be dealt with too harshly. Scientific thinking, scientific investigation, scientific experimentation is, if anything, a matter of trial and error and success. This is the past record of any science, however successful. The science of peace can be no exception. When we shall have done our best in our scientific devotion to peace and have most scrupulously sought out the questions of the highest probability of relevance to peace, we still shall have committed for every success a great many trials. This consideration increases greatly the number of questions in our scientific agenda.

The sense of the vastness of the job increases when we reflect upon the size of our society. Each of us now lives in one and the same world of billions of others. This one world is greater in numbers of human individual entities and is more complex than the world of Alexander the Great or Socrates or Francis Bacon or Abraham Lincoln. For purposes of peace and peace securement, the oneness of the world can be an appalling consideration. Among other things, it means that peace is indivisible. No man dares be an island, nor do any group of men. Modern transportation being what it is, there is no place to go to hide and be peaceful in a world which is not at peace. Peace is indivisible in the sense that an individual in any part of the world has within him the potential of disturbing the peace of any individual anywhere else. Six years before the hydrogen explosion of 1954 in the Pacific, David Bradley wrote in his book, *No Place to Hide*:

> This is not merely academic. Such studies may influence the lives of people living in the Tibetan plateau. We don't know to what distances from Bikini the radiation disease may be carried. We can't predict to what degree the balance of nature will be thrown off by atomic bombs. We certainly have little idea what the long-range effects on our lives would be from an all-out atomic war, devastating our shores, our fish and our agricultural industries. But at least at this time we do know that Bikini is not some faraway little atoll pin-pointed on an out-of-the-way chart. Bikini is San Francisco

Bay, Puget Sound, East River. It is the Thames, the Adriatic, Hellespont, and misty Baikal. It isn't just King Judas and his displaced native subjects about whom we have to think—or to forget.

Now if we accept the notion that war cause and peace foundation are constituted of the kind of stuff that can be found within the minds of men, we have to ask: In which minds? And since we do not know the answer to this question, our research has to concern itself with the minds of all the persons who inhabit the earth. The peace we hope to obtain is a peace among all, and not among a few. We dare not ignore any person. We dare not overlook any mind. This should be our open-minded approach at the outset. Later we may develop priorities of probability.

More than this, since we don't know what is in the mind of any one person, we dare not overlook any part of his mind. A single mind is a tremendously extended and complicated terrain of hopes and fears—of information and misinformation. These facts, fictions, and feelings for any one person may number high up into the thousands if not millions. Which of these are crucial to our problem of war versus peace—extinction versus survival? Since we cannot at the outset tell, we must hold ourselves alert to any portion of man's mental make-up.

So much for the vastness of our task—the multiplicity of the questions we need to answer. This vastness might well be discouraging. Now there are two profoundly important principles of research which, while not abolishing our occasion for concern, do hold the promise of reducing the task to negotiable dimensions. The understanding of their nature and of their applicability to our problem should surely raise our confidence.

The Principle of Sampling

The first of these profoundly important principles is that of sampling.[1] This is one of the greatest discoveries of science in

[1] Many readers will recognize this principle of sampling as incorporated in the widely popularized but much derided public opinion poll movement. The reader is urged here again not to judge the science of the future by the incomplete or even pseudo-science of the past. It is true that in this chapter we are talking about opinion and attitude research. There are a number of limitations and defects to be removed to bring opinion polls to an adequate stage to serve the ends of adequate international understanding. These refer to (a) the motive, i.e., purpose designed to serve, (b) the client, i.e., the total public versus partisan private groups, (c) the secrecy under which conducted (very little of the opinion research done *on* the public is released *to*

general and of social science in particular. According to this principle, it is not necessary to study two billion minds to understand them. We need only to study adequately-sized samples thereof. We conceive two populations—the total population and the sample population. The ratio in size between these two populations in the case of adequate sampling of a large population is of such an order as to strain the credulity of those who are not familiar with the workings of this principle. In fact it is not the ratio but the absolute size of the sample that is critical. As thus far tested, this sampling principle means that a fair notion of what is in the minds of everybody in the world can be had by an intensive study of one person out of 1,000 or 10,000 or possibly one out of 100,000. That is, an intensive study of no more than a million and possibly as few as 25,000 persons could give us the answers we need. Raymond Cattell of Illinois University has projected a study which aims at one in 30,000. These figures are merely indicative. The actual number of samples and thus the total sample size will need to be experimentally determined as the studies proceed.

Now this principle of sampling applies not only to a universe of persons. Its applicability to a universe of material within a given mind or person has been clearly demonstrated. While most of its applicability to the problem of peace has yet to be developed, we can illustrate its operation in connection with other and various measurements of mentality. A very common illustration is its use in measuring a student's knowledge of a subject at the end of a course. Here no teacher would, on examination day, care to ask a question about every point or fact presented over a period of months. He is forced to limit the examination to a sample. The student may contend that the sample is unfair or unrepresentative, but the teacher sticks to sampling.

Many refinements have come with modern measurement in educational psychology. For instance, the vocabulary specialist

the public), (d) the scope and intensity of the investigation. This last point relates to methodology of attitude measurement and analysis which our commercial pollsters have not been in a position to fully develop. The result has been that the fruits of polling have been answers to relatively surface questions whose interpretations involve much controversy. The plan in this chapter involves taking advantage of all we have learned thus far with this amazing but poorly developed instrument and carrying it much further in spite of past mistakes and current low repute. Its possibilities have scarcely been scratched. There must be effective ways of finding out how peoples feel about one another that are not yet discovered.

submits 50 or 100 words and deduces therefrom that person A has a total recognition knowledge of 10,000 words; person B, 12,000; and person C, 15,000. As in population sampling, so in psychological sampling, there are many fine points still at issue, and many areas still unexplored. The validity of the general principle, however, is never questioned by the specialists in psychological measurement. Here, too, and even more so than in population sampling, the accurate and extended application of the principle calls for some honest and earnest research.

In brief, we are proposing that as we seek out the misunderstandings which cause war, our original number-one-level question of how to bring peace will undergo successive stages and levels of sub-division until we get down to the number three level (see Ch. 7) where 100,000 people of all types, descriptions and locations will be asked from 1,000 to 10,000 questions each. If we take the upper limit and multiply the aforesaid 100,000 persons by 10,000 questions, we arrive at the end product of a billion questions. Thus we extremely illustrate the multiplicity of the questions that may need to be asked. The number is great, but now begins to look more finite though still not very negotiable.

The Principle of Division of Labour

A second principle, previously referred to, is that of the division of labour. While it is true that the world in which we live and which has to be studied is a very big world, it is also true that the world from which we are able to draw the students or investigators to make the necessary studies is also this same large world. In this respect, population size is a tremendous asset to science. By the very nature of the process, science is an enterprise involving mutual exchange of knowledge. Science is a co-operative enterprise where the achievement of anyone is dependent upon the success of others who hold the same goal. The individual is privileged to enjoy the fruits of knowledge for which he himself did not pay the initial price. As previously stated, research is only scientific where men search for the kind of knowledge which is transferable from investigator to investigator and eventually to non-investigators. What matters it if we have 100,000 questions requiring answers, if we have 100,000 persons who can divide the labour and each attacks intensively and wholeheartedly a single question? What matters it if the labour required for a science of peace adds up to two million man-years, if we have a million men to share the labour?

However, the division of labour is a treacherous thing. The possibility of a division of labour that is adequate is one thing, and its realization is quite another. The value of the answers depends upon the completeness of the pattern of answers. This means that adequacy of scope of the work of the scientific workers is highly essential. It is of the nature of the scientific operation that science must proceed piece-meal. This is why, as indicated earlier, science is so liable to be partial and tragically incomplete. Widespread criticism of our scientific age is to the effect that men have placed too much faith in science. This criticism contends that science cannot give us all the answers. We agree that science has not given us all the answers. As one scientist has said, 'It has not started to ask many of the questions'. This fact is very serious. Our contention, however, is that the cure for the incompleteness of science is in conscious, deliberate, and planned concern for greater scientific scope. The cure for incomplete science is not something unscientific. The cure is in more science, science with more adequate scope.

At the risk of repetition, let us state that our concern should be at two levels if we would meet the challenge of the present threat of extinction. At the first level of concern the scope of science must be extended to include what we have been referring to here as the science of peace, under whatever name it may come. At the second level of concern the science of peace itself must have sufficient scope to provide all the knowledge necessary to add up to the know-how for peace. If significant knowledge is left out, the result will be fatal. What all these significant knowledges are, no one can now tell, but let us illustrate the possibility of incompleteness. If we know that the failure of the government of nation X to co-operate with nation Y is due to the foreign policy of the officials of nation Y, we will still need to know the cause of the foreign policy of nation Y. This is only one of many types of possible omission.

But how can scope be achieved? We will need to concern ourselves with the proper make-up of teams of scientific workers, and an adequate distribution and co-ordination of thousands of such teams. The workers for the peace of the world will need to be very numerous in order to achieve the scope that is necessary.

Because of this and to achieve the division of labour that we are referring to, the peace scientists will need to group themselves into teams. The make-up of these teams will have to develop as a matter of experience. There are certain features, however, which can be envisioned at the outset as desirable.

Team Structure

In the various research teams there will need to be various kinds of talents, representing different disciplines and different skills. There will be needed hewers of wood and drawers of water as well as creators and tacticians. There will be needed experts in economics as well as political science; statisticians as well as psychologists; persons skilled in the science and art of sampling both from the populational and the psychological point of view; linguists and semanticists, theoreticians and philosophers; men skilled in interviewing and in the use of the numerous and amazing machines which score and record and sort and classify data. A great many types of intellectual passion will be useable.

More important than the diversity of talent, however, is the need for cultural and political inclusiveness. Since peace is a cosmopolitan matter, it will be necessary to have our teams cosmopolitan in make-up. They will need to represent a diversity in terms of background and loyalty (not to say bias) and understanding (not to say misunderstanding). If we are studying the opinions of the citizens of one country toward all other countries, and interpreting the relationship of these opinions to realities that exist in these other countries, it would seem highly desirable that the interpreters include citizens from all countries. This we realize is an ideal which may be handicapped in its operation by various factors, including the dearth of individuals unobstructed by the barriers of language and other cultural fences.

Our goal should be cosmopolitan teams composed of cosmopolitan members. Calling attention to both the importance and the difficulty of this feature of world-mindedness, Stuart Chase asks:

Where are the men who can transcend their own cultures and really labour in the Lord's vineyard serving mankind ? There are a few at Lake Success, but most delegates seem never to have thought of the distinction. They assume they are there to represent their country's interest, to see that nothing is put over on Ruritania. It is probable that the U N will never amount to much until delegates begin to see this cardinal distinction and think in terms of 'mankind first, my country second.'

Under the circumstances, what else can we expect? If one represents a partisan political client, one is more likely to function partisanly. We must seek to change the circumstances. Since the goal of this research is total peace, peace for all men, the sponsorship should be as wide as possible. If there is to be supervision or review of methods of the science of peace by a commission, the more widely representative this commission be of all nations and of all classes, the better.

Similarly, the wider the support, the better. Within limits, the poor as well as the rich might be privileged to pay the piper. A supporting budget coming from citizens of all nations would be more ideal than one drawn from one nation. A supporting fund administered or distributed through the U N would be better than one exclusively controlled by the government of the U.S.A. or the U.S.S.R. or Britain or India, etc., at least while suspicion abounds and armament research and cold psychological warfare continue.

Another factor that must be kept in mind from the point of view of adequate scope is that there be different teams to test out different, and sometimes contradictory hypotheses. This is one of the fascinating features of the scientific movement. A science of human relations need not ask men to abandon their ideological convictions. Progress towards harmony is in the promise to subject our differences to careful and honest investigation. It is not possible in actual procedure for a given nation to practise simultaneously the principles of armament and disarmament. It is possible, however, for teams of scientists sponsored by a given nation or a given set of nations to investigate and pursue scientific research concurrently on armament and disarmament possibilities. Without waiting for nations to break their habits of doing research on making weapons more potent and deadly, we can start doing research on how to make weapons unnecessary and undesired. We propose disarmament *research* as the real antidote to the toxic processes of the armament race.

Finally, since science is not only organized intelligence, but creative intelligence as well, and thrives under freedom, the ideal would seem to be organization and co-ordination from the bottom up rather than from the top down. No single bureau or commission should have the power to throttle the research of sincere, creative individuals, however much the latter might seem to be out of step with other workers in the same or different areas. It is one of the characteristics of science that it thrives under freedom and with multiplicity of hypotheses. This ideal of democratic relationship will require that large quantities of real intelligence be invested to devise and operate more and more adequate techniques for inter-communication among scientists and between the scientists and the people.

Dividing the Labour

Let us now look at some examples of how the labour might be divided. For a science of peace we must conceive a division of labour whereby the manpower organizes and distributes itself so that nothing is ignored—no facet of the human mind or personality pertinent to peace, and no sociological group or geographic location of minds in its potential relationship to peace. The two first major approaches to the division of labour which are suggested in the following pages illustrate how these features might be systematically approached. These might be called the Populational Approach and the Psychological Approach.

The reader is asked to keep in mind throughout the following illustrations two conditions:

1. The primary purpose of our planning is to avoid, not duplication but gaps or omissions in the process. We must say that an undertaking which is geared to survival cannot afford to be also geared to economy *per se*.

2. All of these illustrations must be taken as tentative. They are suggestions merely, and will be modified or abandoned if and as large numbers of highly creative men are put to work designing and implementing a science of peace.

The Populational Approach

Let us consider first the question: Where must a science of peace look for those understandings relevant to war and peace? In what minds? In what geographic locations? In what sociologic groups? In what zones of educational influence? In spite of all statements of how little our world has become, it is still a big world in which men with minds are as widely scattered as ever. If all are to be adequately represented in a serious study, a study as serious as one related to the issue of survival versus extinction, no portion of the earth should be overlooked. No sociologically or educationally differentiated segment of society should be ignored. If there should exist a small *élite* in whose minds the preponderant influence operates, this fact must be guardedly ascertained and not guessed at.

A. GEOGRAPHICAL DISTRIBUTION OF WORKERS

One way to increase the probability of complete coverage is through geographical division. There might well be a team of investigators *for* each nation. This is in line with the hypothesis that international conflict versus international harmony is a function of international attitude.

Depending upon the total number in our society who devote themselves to a science of peace, we might compromise on the number of separate teams. Certain nations which have much in common in terms of language and culture might be grouped. If the programme of research should expand steadily but not very rapidly, the first studies might better be plotted in those nations where the virulence of violence seems most probable. Far better, however, than to limit the areas of inspection through the crude necessities of limited manpower would be the development in which decisions were progressively based upon experimental findings. Thus it might be found that the number of regions, political and otherwise, which need to be studied separately are not so great as we have indicated. Our contention here is not for the precise number of geographically organized teams but for the principle that separate teams are needed for separate jobs, teams cosmopolitan in make-up and yet differing from one another in their language skills, and in their cultural and historical understandings.

As we have suggested, it might be possible as time goes on to combine certain geographic or national groups. On the other hand, it may become necessary, upon closer inspection and as the manpower permits, to sub-divide the labour in each regional or national group. Each national or regional team would have a complex task. For instance, a team to study the attitudes of the

British toward the French, and also toward the Russians, Indians, Arabians, etc. We might look forward to an International attitude graph that will tell us on each of a number of counts the attitude for each of 70 or 80 nations: (1) its attitude toward and understanding of each of the other nations; and (2) the attitude of each of the other nations toward it. If, for instance, the attitude of Swedes or Italians towards the U.S. is different from that of Mexicans or of Philippinos, we may have much food for prediction as to how rapport between nations generally can be favourably effected.

It must be recalled that our contention here is not that nothing has ever been done about this sort of thing, but that so little has been done, especially with rigorous scientific care, and with global perspective. The urgent need is that in the future our discussions and our thinking be based on solid scientific observation of the feelings of people toward one another throughout the world. Distinct advances have been made in scientific technique under partisan auspices. The author knows of one agency well financed by one nation and exclusively concerned with studying opinion in a few other nations. These findings are rarely released to the public within any nation.

If we are to catch up quickly with the misunderstandings that are bedevilling our relations internationally, we must take seriously the requisite size of these national teams. They might vary from 100 to 1,000 or more workers per nation. The need for this expansion becomes more apparent as we pass now to our next step. Continuing our distribution of teams according to population, our second concern is for covering all sociologic groups within a geographic area.

B. SOCIOLOGICAL DISTRIBUTION OF WORKERS

Even though we study separately the attitude of the Japanese toward the Russian, or the attitude of the Russian toward the British, we would want to break down these by sociological groups. We must not ignore differences between farmers and city dwellers, between the privileged and the underprivileged, the literate and the illiterate. There is need for expert teams for dealing with the psychology of differentiated groups: white-collar groups, blue-collar groups, etc.—professional people, skilled people, semi-skilled people—political people and non-political—office holders

OUTLINING THE RESEARCH   131

and private citizens—young people, old people, male and female —more religious and less religious. All these need to be studied somewhat distinctly throughout the world.

This division of workers to attend to sociologically differentiated types is here considered sub-divisional to the geographic. For example, if there be 70 nations and 20 sociologically differentiated teams in each, we would have 1,400 teams with much overlap in their goal and with need for co-operation in their search.

C. DISTRIBUTION OF WORKERS TO TRACE EDUCATIONAL INFLUENCE

As teams envisioned under the preceding sections (A and B) seek to ascertain what significant inter-nation attitudes are now present, it could be the business of teams in this third category to attempt to account for the origin and nurture of these attitudes. Here our key question is: What are the institutional processes of education and propaganda which are fostering the attitudes and the differences in attitudes in the various nations and in the various classes within nations? Moreover, what are their effects upon what types of persons and by virtue of what operations? Customarily listed as primarily educational are such institutions as the school, the church, and the family. In addition to these we would need to take account of other sources including (a) mass communication (wireless, press, movies), and (b) other points of communication such as office, factory, farm, playground, tavern, and library, as well as fraternal, labour, commercial and social and political groups.

The pattern of educational agencies will vary, of course, from nation to nation. In the U.S.A. the big three are often assumed to be the wireless (radio and T V), the press, and the movies. Here again we have some of the pieces of scientific work, but they are neither sufficient nor sufficiently combined. Serious beginnings have already been made in analysing programmes of these agencies. The research on content analysis must be closely related with audience response, audience development and audience selection of attention. We need to note not only what people hear or see, but with what emotional and intellectual and overt response. We need to know not only what men listen to, but who listens to what and why. Millions of dollars have already been paid by commercial agencies to commercial agencies for the measurement of audience response. The purpose has been to predict box office profits. Practically nothing has been done to measure mass media potency for developing goodwill at the international level. Is education defaulting on this ideal? How much? Where and how and why?

The guiding purpose in our thinking about a populational division of labour is to avoid skipping any significantly different segment of our total human population whether separated by political or geographic or sociologic or educational boundary lines. We cannot take chances on fatal omissions of some of the types of minds in which wars are made. Let us turn now to the problem of including all of mind so as not to skip any significant part of the psychology of the individual.

The Psychological Approach

If society is a bundle of persons, a person is a bundle of attitudes. Whereas the population approach asks, '*Who* believes what?' the psychological approach asks, 'What does who believe?' The psychological approach is the more difficult. We have presented the populational first because it is simpler and more obvious. We know more about the topography of the earth than we know about the psychology of the individual. The psychological approach should not be considered as alternative to the populational approach, but as complementary. To illustrate this approach to the division of labour, we now wish to present four fairly distinct formulations.

A. studies of political motivation

Why do people behave politically as they do? How can we explain the political behaviour of individuals within nations, behaviour which is conducive to war and behaviour which is conducive to peace?

Whatever the underlying cause of inter-nation conflict and inter-nation co-operation, two things need to be said at the more easily observable levels. One is that the final acts which initiate a period of open and violent strife consist of the acts of political figures—prime ministers, secretaries of state and of 'defence'. The second thing is that political actors in the drama of history not only act but are acted upon. Their behaviour to be understood must be studied in terms of a process of interaction, including the actions and the expected actions of others. These others include not only persons on the opposite side of the diplomatic screen, but also individuals on the same side. These individuals on the same side consist not only of fellow office holders, other members of cabinets and political bureaus; they include the non-governmental and non-official, not only the great and near-great, but common men as well. The ascertainment of this interaction, the weights of the various types of persons, official and unofficial, may well be one of the objectives of a science of peace.

The organization of workers for this objective may be by nations. That is, workers might concentrate on particular nations for which their interest, experience and specific training especially fit them. We are aware that volumes have been written in an attempt to explain national behaviour and international conflict in this manner. We submit that these analyses, though sometimes brilliant, are seldom if ever fed by an adequate and sufficient amount of pertinent data to explain adequately the motive behind the motive, behind the act, which preceded the act.

What are the facts about political motivation for continuing war preparation? What motives inhibit officials from initiating arrangements or processes which might lead to the cessation of war preparation? On the one hand, the story is told of a journalist approaching a very high U.S.A. official and urging him to call an international conference for the purpose of strengthening the United Nations. The official said, 'It wouldn't do any good. The people would not support me'. Unfortunately, here the story ends. On the other hand, the writer has interviewed scores of USans on the problem of world unity who say, 'There is nothing we ordinary people can do. The people up at Washington will pay no attention to us'. How can we check the validity of these beliefs? Will the people in high position be returned to office or retired by the voters if their behaviour toward other nations is more co-operative and less 'tough'? Is the high official being motivated by what he has heard from the grass roots, or by a threat or a promise or a piece of advice from some unofficial leader? Or have both the people and the official been influenced by the opinions, not to say the whims, of some unidentified leader of opinion?

B. IDEO-GENETIC STUDIES

What is the origin and development of ideas? Where do our beliefs come from? Are some ideas which are highly related to war or peace also highly related to each other? Are these related to ideas which appear to have no relation to war and peace?

There are those who say that thoughts have a life and a history of their own; that they are born and grow; spread throughout a population or certain areas or levels of population; and on occasion contract and wither. During World War II some interesting and exciting projects were carried on in the U.S.A. under the title of Rumor Clinics, in which 'myths' unfavourable to the morale of the country and its winning of the war were studied. Somewhat successful attempts were made to trace these rumours, if not to their original source, at least to some of their secondary sources. If we are right in believing that wars are caused by misunderstandings, it may be possible to undermine the institution of war by carefully guided observations that will lead to identification not only of the misunderstandings which facilitate conflict and endanger the peace but also their sources.

Such a study as here proposed would be curious about the kinship among ideas. What kind of company does a given idea keep? For instance, is the idea that Japanese are highly and relatively suicidal in the presence of patriotic motivation more likely to be found in the same mind as certain ideas about Negroes having a higher sense of humour than whites, etc?

Further, one might study the route which an idea takes in its line of transmission. It would seem feasible to ask the possessor of a particular idea to name other individuals who, to his knowledge, have the same opinion or from whom he first received it. In this way the course of an idea from person to person might be traced. Such a project as this might develop profound knowledge about the natural order of expansion of an idea, not only as it spreads to ever greater numbers of persons, but as it evolves, especially in its elements of contradiction, to ascertainable fact. Would such evolution follow different or similar patterns in different subcultures?

C. STUDIES OF PERSONALITY CONTRASTS

What characteristics in general differentiate the world-minded from the nationally-minded? Those whose loyalties and sympathies are more world-wide, more attached to human and global symbols, and those more narrow in their sympathies and attachments?

We assume that the beliefs which are pertinent to the issue of peace vary from person to person, and not only in kind but in amount; that individuals as individuals vary in the extent to which they can be eventually shown to be assets or liabilities for the peace of the world; and that in part at least this is a matter of personality. We pose this question in this way because there is implied in it an operational extension in terms of an intensive, objective comparison of specific, living, accessible individuals.

Such contrasted studies to reveal the correlates of peace-mindedness need to be made as quickly as possible in every type of community or culture now existent. It may well be that such study will throw light upon the question as to whether war or peace and their causes are the same the world around, or to the extent to which this is true, and the number and types of exceptions which have to be made to any generalization about war causation. This method or type of project has the advantage that it can be conducted anywhere at any time by any appreciably sized research staff without waiting for comparable staffs to be started elsewhere.

D. BASIC PERSONALITY ANALYSIS

What are the basic traits of personality? How are they related to peace and to war?

A woefully small amount of serious psychological research has been devoted to the basic task of the objective measurement and analysis of the attitudes of individuals. An expansion of the idea of personality contrast study just described would largely develop into a programme of basic personality analysis. Under the former we would assume sufficient initial insight to separate and thus contrast world-minded and nationally-minded persons. Most students of personality structure and growth, however, would freely admit that we have barely scratched the surface of knowledge in this area. Profound and wide-scale approaches are in order.

Essential to the understanding of individual personality is an understanding of the interactions of individuals with one another. Questions must be asked about the differences between personality traits and behaviours of individuals within a group, and about the relationship of these differences to the interactions between or among groups or cultures or nations.

The job of psychological analysis requires highly developed tools for measurement. There is little scientific value in being able to say that some people are more happy than others if the happy and the unhappy remain unidentified. It is hardly the highest level of understanding to say that the behaviour of this individual interacts with, or influences, or is influenced by, the behaviour of that individual, unless and until we can generalize and say what types of personality interact how and under what conditions. This brings us to the problem of methodology.

Method Research

At the risk of oversimplification, we might say that each of the two different major approaches which we have tentatively set up hinges upon a different key word. In the case of the populational approach, the word is: *Where?* Where should the peace scientist look for that which is relevant to war and peace? In whose minds? In the case of the psychological approach, the word is: *What?* What shall the scientist look for? What kind of psychological material? Now with methodology, we might conceive the key word to be: *How?* How can we best find out the kind of things we need to find out to arrive at the know-how for peace? Not, where or what are they, but by what methods can we most speedily ascertain them? In contrast to other enterprises, the scientific enterprise is unique in its relatively great emphasis on method (as developed in Article 4. Chapter 6).

While method will be of some concern to all major sections of a peace research staff, it should be the special concern of a special division. Such a division would not be responsible for finding out the truth about human attitudes of peace, but would be free to use their time unreservedly for finding out *how* to find out; for testing methods; for creating new approaches.

A very important feature of method improvement in science is that which relates to methods or techniques or tools for measure-

OUTLINING THE RESEARCH

ment. Sooner or later the scientist has to go beyond the limitations of an all-or-none approach to the qualities which confront him. Eventually the questions of quantity become overpowering. To the ever-present questions of 'What?' there have to be added the questions of 'How much?' Science develops with the development of its instruments for making measured observations. Witness the vast array of measuring instruments, thermometers, barometers, micrometers, voltmeters, altimeters, chronometers, psychometers, etc.

The impulse to study human attitudes experimentally has had no greater block than that which comes from our feeling of inability to measure cause and evaluate outcome. A popular argument against the scientific study of attitudes holds that they are intangible and hence not subject to quantitative scrutiny. We submit that the business of science is to bring the intangible progressively into the realm of the tangible. Note what has happened to the tangibility of the speed of light, blood pressure, microscopic bacteria, to say nothing of the formerly intangible, unseeable, unhearable radio waves which carry symphonic music over oceans and mountains, and the various dimensions of bolts of lightning which our barbarian forebears dared not touch. Deprive the electronic engineer of his testing gadgets and he would resign. Comparable progress in the field of attitude study requires a generous allotment of scientific workers to this phase of the problem. Too long have the students in this area soft-pedalled the need of this phase of science. As George Lundberg says:

It is comparatively easy to get a hundred thousand dollars for a social survey of a local community if immediate results of value are thought probable. It is very difficult to get a fraction of that sum for research on the development of social measuring instruments, for example. Yet the latter, when developed, become the principal means of reliable and economical 'practical' research as well as the chief means for the advance of science. The matter can perhaps be summarized most briefly by imagining what would be the state of knowledge, research and practical efficiency in the physical sciences if every researcher had to invent anew for each research project, instruments for the measurement of time, length, weight, temperature, etc. The corresponding state of affairs is virtually what today exists in the social sciences. There is no systematic theory which stipulates what we choose to regard as fundamental dimensions of social behaviour and there are few standardized and verifiable definitions and measures of the various concepts and dimensions used by various researchers. Deliberate and co-ordinated work on this key problem might properly engage some of the attention of research foundations interested in fundamental research.

(Social Research, pp. 33–34)

Such a project or division of labourers on methodology *per se* should have the resources to survey critically all methods current at any given time. It would involve the labour of many types of talent—experts in the field of biochemistry, in mathematics, in electrical engineering, involving automatic tabulating, computing and calculating machinery. It would consist of a division of labourers to which any individual engaged in any other aspect of peace research could turn in time of technical difficulty.

But this question of methodology, we believe, should be viewed in a broad sense, so that it includes more than the goal of ever-increasing accuracy and sensitivity of our tools or techniques or instruments of measurement and observation. It should also include the aim of increasing freedom and objectivity for the scientific observers. From this point of view it is in order to ask: By what methods or arrangements can we secure suitable conditions for free and unbiased research? For one thing, how can we minimize the dangers of the bias of the observers and the interpreters, and the designers as well? Gunnar Myrdal says that 'radicalism and conservatism is the master scale of bias in the social sciences'. The radical minded and the conservative naturally desire to prove different and often contradictory hypotheses. They are tempted to choose different problems or aspects of a problem. They are liable to make different interpretation or generalization from the same data. This is a heavy challenge to those of us who believe in a science of human relations. Experts on scientific method should be able to develop ways of meeting this challenge. They should become experts in objectification of the study of human values. They should neither fear nor evade this problem.

Other Illustrations of Division of Labour

We pause to remind the reader that our discussions in this chapter are for the sake of illustrating how the labour might be organized or divided. The foregoing proposals, even if adopted in their entirety, do not exclude dozens of other approaches, any of which can be used to supplement the picture we have thus far drawn, and might eventually if not immediately supplant the plan of organization herein suggested. We wish now to suggest some of these other approaches. There will be a temptation to think of them as minor approaches and as supplements rather than illustrations. Since, however, they are as yet of an embryonic nature, we should approach them creatively, not forgetting that they may have possibilities of great expansion.

A. ORGANIZATION OF TEAMS OF ALREADY ESTABLISHED SPECIALISTS

We should make special effort to utilize whatever social science knowledge and skill is now available. Workers and thinkers from particular disciplines tend to develop language of their own. They can more easily work out their solutions in contact with their fellow-thinkers. The danger, however, is that if philosophers or economists do work out a solution, they may do so in a language which is not intelligible to the outsider. This is not the fault of working together. It is the fault of not going far enough to the point where they can fit the efforts and the fruits of their work into the thinking and research of other scientists and into the feeling and action of other citizens. The case for the divisions we are about to suggest can be made only on the assumption of adequate orientation of each group and adequate contact among the groups which make the various approaches:

1. *The Philosophers*

There is a general theory among many cynics that philosophy 'pumps no water', 'bakes no bread'. The extent that this has been true in the past may be due to either of two attitudinal misfortunes. Either the philosophers have not been interested in bread and water, or the philosophers and the other members of the total pumping and baking team have not been in proper communication or articulation with each other. Here as elsewhere we believe we cannot afford to condemn a type of service entirely on its failure to date. Rather we must look at possibilities of what a type worker might conceivably accomplish with certain changes of method or emphasis or direction. We like John Dewey's note of optimism:

Philosophy still has a work to do. It may gain a role for itself for turning to consideration of why it is that man is now so alienated from man. It may turn to the projections of large generous hypotheses which, if used as plans of actions, will give intelligent direction to men in search for ways to make the world more one of worth and significance, more homelike, in fact. There is no phase of life, educational, economic, political, religious, in which inquiry may not aid in bringing to birth that world which Matthew Arnold rightly said was as yet unborn. Present day philosophy cannot desire a better work than to engage in the act of midwifery that was assigned to it by Socrates 2500 years ago.

(Problems of Men, p. 20)

We believe that there need be no hard and fast boundary-line between philosophy and scientific experimentation. Rather there should be an interaction between hypothesis and verification; between theorizing and data gathering. It is conceivable that had there been an adequate balance and co-operation between the philosopher and the scientist in the past 200 years, we would not be in our present predicament. It is not hard to argue that science is breaking down at the higher echelons of social theory. The ill effect of compartmentalization within the individual mind as well as within the intellectual community have to be acknowledged. But greater integration can be our legitimate goal.

2. *The Historians and Political Scientists*

What we have said regarding philosophy applies equally much to history and political science. Our guess is that both have defaulted regarding the larger issues—history because it has not been concerned with the future; political science because it has not been sufficiently concerned with the larger political unit. Whatever we may say about history for history's sake, we can at least experimentally and tentatively suggest the study of history for the sake of peace. The space given in departments of political science in many universities to consideration of city government, county government, state government, and national government is shocking in comparison to the space given to world government or even so-called international law. If political scientists have been concerned with institutions rather than men, with the structure of government and not psychological motivation, and if history has been too much concerned with big men and not enough with common men, why cannot correction be made? Cannot both of these disciplines help the philosophers draw somewhat 'large and generous hypotheses' suitable for check by other disciplines or if necessary by totally new disciplines?

3. *The Economists*

What a pathos if those people are right who say that war's cause and war's cure is to be found in economics, but we fail to put economists to work on the job, adequate and sufficient to ascertain the full truth in time. In the later nineteenth century, William James conceived the need for *A Moral Equivalent for War*. Had he lived in the mid-twentieth century he might well have conceived the need for an economic equivalent for war. Do men fear peace for economic reasons? Do we need a world monetary system? Is it possible at the present moment? What preliminary changes will form an effective approach thereto? Is the International Trade Organization ill-fated? Are there simple facts about the economy of specific nations or the psychology of the peoples therein which are blocking the progress of I T O, and which need to be ascertained and made known? What are the psychological factors behind the phenomenon of tariffs? What stands in the way of tariff reform? Again may we suggest that if economists have not made their contribution to peace, may it be because of faulty direction and emphasis due to inadequate allocation of scientific workers to this specific need? There are a great many thousands of economists attached to the executive branches of our national governments. A great many more are attached to the high commands of our great corporations and cartels. These are committed by virtue of the ethics of their loyalties to study economics from the point of view of a part of humanity. What might not an appreciable portion of them accomplish if mandated by society as a whole!

What we have said about special groups or teams for philosophy, history, political science, or economics can be said about many other disciplines, such as anthropology, psychology, sociology, psychiatry, semantics, etc. For the operation of any such team, the clear requirements seem two-fold: (1) that there be sufficient support in terms of money-power making possible the necessary manpower; (2) that the concern for the discipline for its own sake be such as to allow optimal concern for peace. For instance, if our enthusiasm for a science of peace shall fail to develop optimally the science of anthropology but at the same time bring us inter-nation peace and survival, there will be a chance to develop this and many other sciences later. On the other hand, if we develop anthropology or any other discipline, but fail to secure peace and hence survival, it shall profit us nothing.

B. ORGANIZATION FROM THE POINT OF VIEW OF SPECIFIC OBJECTIVES OR SPECIAL ENTHUSIASMS

The movement for world peace as any other movement of importance needs to capitalize as far as possible the enthusiasms or spiritual resources connected with a wide array of approaches. It should be a first principle in the economy of peace or peace research to alienate no one who has any possibility of making a contribution, however oblique. It is sometimes difficult to separate an individual's enthusiasm for peace from his enthusiasm for a particular method in which he has faith. To start with, it might make little difference as to whether the faith is justified, providing one can proceed with open-minded alertness toward his specific end and a wholesome degree of scepticism and creative attitude toward the appropriate means of reaching it. In social pathology almost any remedy might eventually prove to have an appreciable amount of real validity if appropriately modified. The following four illustrations we think provide a wide variety.

1. *World Government*

The writer has been impressed with the extraordinary sincerity and enthusiasm of many of the world government proponents whom he has met. The impression always continues, however, that here is a place where the good intentions have not been good enough. Costly conflict and paralysing frustration too often occur. Much of the waste and frustration and loss of morale might well have been avoided if some of the heat could have been transformed into additional light. To many of us it is difficult to conceive of real peace without disarmament and hence without world order and hence without world law and hence without world government. But law and government democratically conceived is a matter of broad co-operation and consensus. How is this consensus to be achieved? What are the anchor posts in the minds of men on which a true political concurrence can be constructed? Here we are at the heart of the scientific problem of human unity.

2. Universal Language

Not every one feels the need for a common language. Still fewer are the people who believe it feasible in any reasonable length of time, but there seems to be a spirit favourable to world unity among Esperantists and those who have learned other auxiliary languages or reflect over the amazing handicap to our much needed intercommunication by our multiplicity of tongues. Here again any professional study from this approach would eventually (and inevitably) lead us into inquiry into attitudes related to world unity. Many persons have suggested universalization of English as the solution. But all these people now speak English.

3. Religion

Among those who refer to religion as a crucial phenomenon in the matter of world peace, it is sometimes difficult to separate those who are interested in peace and those who are merely interested in religion (or in a particular religion). Here as with other subjects such as history and economics we do not believe that religion for religion's sake can be counted upon to bring us peace. Perhaps there are numerous persons who have coupled with their great conviction for religion a real and serious scientific curiosity regarding the limitations of religion—curiosity regarding its failure thus far to turn the tide against ethical barbarism. Such persons might well believe there could be great profit in the scientific study of the role of religion in the development of brotherhood at the political and global level. How can we hope to ascertain and change its negative or positive role in the face of our current ignorance—an ignorance attested by widespread disagreement and contradiction? Surely here is a task to challenge the utmost effort and skill of men with warm hearts and cool heads.

4. Transnational Inter-community Contact and Contrast Studies

We are using the word community here to cover such entities as a village or city or university or more closely-knit sub group thereof. For instance, two university classes or faculties in different nations or continents might carry on intensive, protracted, guided, group correspondence. Such interaction might furnish a possibility of hitting upon procedures for progressively revealing international and intercultural misunderstandings, and overcoming them. Small beginnings in this direction have been made in several programmes not set up for research purpose. One of these is the school affiliation programme promoted by the American Friends Service Committee.

C. ACTION RESEARCH

There are those who argue for a certain concept, namely action research, as representing something required in social science over and above what seems to be effective in physical science. This position was represented by an organization recently which adopted the slogan—No research without action, and no action without research. It is an intriguing concept. The big problem is not in the theoretical validity of the conception, but in the refinements for actually bringing about this merging of service and science in one and the same project. Our observation has been that, of the two, it is much harder to meet the requirements and avoid the deflections of the research. Always the research is pushed aside by the greater compulsion of the practical demands of the service. Then too there is the great danger of mixing the implicit moral values of the investigator with his research findings. The cure here is not less action research but more that is more profound and objective. We wish to clarify this idea with three illustrations—one which has had a considerable currency but little research, one with more research, and one which exists only in our imagination.

1. *International Work Camps*

Already some millions of work-hours have been put in by young people in countries of which they are not citizens. Much of this has been carried on under the supervision of such an organization as the Friends Service Committee. These projects have been carried on largely by persons whose interest and confidence in the programme arises out of some sort of religious or ethical inspiration, or general theoretical consideration. It seems that nowhere has there been any check upon such operations as to indicate with clarity and in quantitative terms the effect upon the total international climate. It would be especially desirable to know how much of this sort of experience it might take to bring us peace, and to have trustworthy calculations of the probability of enlisting enough work campers to meet the demands of stemming the tide of international conflict. The idea is appealing. Much of the theory seems sound. We need more facts.

2. *Group Dynamics Movement*

It is assumed that groups have or can have a dynamic existence. It is believed that certain principles governing the processes of group activity and group development can be located and formulated and verified and used for group guidance. A number of short, intensive experiments have been carried on, as at Bethel, Maine, U.S.A., under the leadership of the Instiute for Group Dynamics, in the interests of understanding the principles which control group behaviour. Similar to other spots in the field of social relations there is here an ocean of insights or partial insights into group activity, but there is a dearth of observers and of students to enable us to learn in relatively meaningful terms just what goes on and who or what is responsible for the success or non-success of particular groups. When the facts of group dynamics are fully revealed we should be able to explain the successes and the failures of groups all the way from a cosmopolitan club on a college campus to the Security Council of the United Nations. The problem of world peace includes the problem of utilizing differences, minimizing conflicts, and harmonizing purposes of the members of any group which functions or might function for world peace. Since so much of human welfare depends upon successful group living, guesswork in this area should be ended as soon as possible.

3. *The Peace College Experiment*

It has been said that the peace movement is stymied because it is 'led by amateurs'. With respect to other goals of our corporate life, we recognize the need to have special training for special function. Those responsible for the future health of the world congregate and prepare themselves in schools of medicine throughout the world. Those who expect to build bridges, dynamos, skyscrapers, highways, factories, and industrial processes congregate in schools of engineering. For those who are, or might be, responsible for the peace of the world, there is no special college or university or school. We have schools for barbers, for bookkeepers, and for motor-mechanics, but no schools where people can become expert in the problem or the problems of peace.

When one considers the multitude of answers and ideas and conflicting theories which one meets in the course of a short time of asking people what they think or what they intend to do about peace, one is impressed with two things: (1) that there are no experts on peace; (2) that there can be no hope for peace without experts. There would seem good logic for staging an experiment which might throw some light on this issue of whether we need special experts on the processes of peace, and whether a specialized teaching and research centre could give promise of supplying such experts. Much theorizing needs to be done to clarify this issue, but in the last analysis, we need the evidence of numerous actual experiments. Such experiments might have to break new ground educationally in many respects. These could be varied from centre to centre. Among other things we would want to know the possibilities and difficulties of assembling successfully individuals from many nations into one institution; an institution in which no one was *foreigner* and no one was *native*. Would it be possible for students of such an institution to find places of participation in the educational and the political and the scientific world? What chance would such graduates have of registering their impact upon the total problem of total peace?

All these experiments would need to be conducted on an intense and follow-through basis. It is not enough to say that Mary Brown and John Jones enjoyed their trip for three months to a work camp in another country. We would need to know how John or Mary behaved a year later; three years later; as well as something of the behaviour of the people with whom John and Mary associated while abroad. How about the behaviour of those contacted after their return? We need to remember that no experiment is complete if there be no measurement at the end.

D. THE NON-SCIENTIFIC OR NEO-SCIENTIFIC APPROACHES

It is possible that when a billion or ten billion man-hours have been invested at intelligent search for the know-how for peace, the kind of finding as well as the kind of procedure for achieving it may come to be very different from what the thinkers of greatest insight and foresight can now anticipate. The science of the future might merit the caption, neo-scientific. We should put no restrictions upon the operation of true intelligence, sincerely devoted to solving the problem of war and extinction versus peace and survival. What these so-called neo-scientific approaches are to be, we cannot here intimate. For instance, there are those who say (vaguely we believe) that the approach may not be by science but by intuition. We believe in so-called intuition as an aid to science. We believe in imagination, in creative intelligence. We believe in releasing it for peace. We want no thoughtless restrictions upon it. If somebody by intuition gets an insight or an idea for peace, we want it released. We believe, however, that we are in an era where theories and thoughts can be tested. We find our progress in those areas where notions and ideas, both new and old, are submitted to careful test. In some form or other all solutions proposed for the problem of war will have to be tested. If there is then a form of checking these ideas or of testing them which is acceptable to the sober intelligence of mankind, we would favour it even if eventually someone does not wish to call it scientific. We believe, however, that most likely the so-called non-scientific approaches or proposals will be incomplete as techniques and will require some testing of a very rigid and objective sort.

General Considerations

We wish to make three general points about plotting the attack upon the ignorance of how to get rid of war. The first is that there are many avenues of approach. There is at present no one, and only one, right way to begin. The important thing is to begin. We quote Alexander Leighton:

The work at the Poston Relocation Centre provided a useful lesson in this regard. At the very beginning the Director asked me to find out how he should handle a small but unruly group of men, 'the old bachelors', who had formerly been itinerant farm labourers. With the problem still before me of getting to know the whole camp of some 20,000 people this seemed incidental and superficial, a question brought up merely because it happened to be the Director's worry for that day. It appeared that tackling it would delay getting at those main dynamic forces in the camp which had to be understood before any real work could be accomplished. Consequently, I did not pick up the Director's question.

A year and a half later, after something had become known about the Centre, it was evident that if I had begun with this unruly group and proceeded in a thoroughgoing manner following all the important interconnections, I would have come rapidly to one of the main dynamic forces of Poston and would have gained a fairly comprehensive picture of the others. It could have been a first-rate problem with which to begin.

This illustrates two sub-points. One is that we should not split too many hairs as to the right way to begin. The second is that no way will be the right way if our efforts are too feeble, and the manpower be too few. Note that Leighton says, 'With the problem still before me...' With the lateness of the hour when Mr. Leighton was called in, and considering the undeveloped state of the science he represented, it is tragic and unbelievable that he should have been given so little force.

Another general consideration that we wish to present is that the plan for a division of labour must be fluid. It must evolve as the research proceeds. Scientific research is a gamble with the unknown. The newness element is relatively great. He who designs or plans a building has or can have the benefit of previously tested and proved plans. Millions of physical structures have been previously built. On the other hand, those who seek to fashion a new scientific structure are, relatively speaking, required to imagine something 'new under the sun'. Planning here has to be learned as the structure evolves. The only way to learn is to plan and test and then plan and test some more.

In the third place, the making of the plan is a part, a necessary and to some extent the early part, of the research itself. Many people foolishly take the position that the planning is preliminary to the research; that the plans must be made and completed before the research begins, and more seriously still, before we even decide to have the research. People frequently say, 'Show us a good plan and then we will support your research'. The cold facts are that research planners have to eat while they plan. Time for planning is part of the tooling-up process. To ignore this is fatal. Good planning requires TIME—and a certain freedom from necessity for haste. Here as elsewhere haste and speed may be highly incompatible.

Conclusion

Let us review. Although real beginnings have been made in research on public opinion and in the measurement of attitude of individuals and the study of group characteristics, these beginnings are but a scratch on the surface. They betoken, however, enormous possibilities for understanding the dynamic factors in men's minds. Such possibilities require favourable circumstances, however, for continuation, and must be channelled seriously toward the problem of world peace. In Chapter 6 it was indicated that there is nothing magical about the method of science. It is merely man taking seriously his propensity to ask, and procure answers to, questions. That there is nothing peculiar about the problem of peace in this respect is shown by the readiness with which many sensible people can ask earnest and intelligent questions when properly challenged.

The purpose of this chapter has been to raise the question: Are the chances of answerability of these questions sufficient to satisfy the conditions of science and the demands of the problem? The multiplicity of our questions, though great, is negotiable if we utilize the principles of sampling and division of labour among an adequate number of teams of workers, distributing themselves well enough to achieve an adequately broad scope to the science of peace. This is providing we can achieve cooperation on a sufficiently wide basis involving a sufficient number of intelligent and concerned scientists and supporters of scientists.

Science does not have to be a menace to survival. By design and deliberation of an intelligent and responsible society, it can be operated as a positive factor for the protection and continuation of the civilization which it has nurtured and by which it has been nurtured. Science has been accused of being atomistic, mechanistic, materialistic, and partialistic. It is time now for those who believe in science to accept the challenge that its frontiers are endless and that nothing real needs to be foreign to science, and most of all nothing human. Herein lies our hope for a much needed scientific humanism which cannot be complete without humanistic science, that is, science by, of, and for people.

9
SPEED AND MANPOWER

> It is certain that if there is any time left in which to alter an otherwise downward course, it is very, very short....
> This means that one can no longer work in problems of human relations, either in big issues or in small, with the feeling that any progress made, however minute, is something gained. An inch made is not now an inch gained. No progress is of value unless it adds up to crossing soon the threshold between things as they are now and a world order in which there will be no war.
>
> ALEXANDER LEIGHTON

IN this chapter we wish to deal with two very practical considerations which cause many persons to hesitate to accept the logic of a science of peace. They ask two questions: Is there time? Are men available?

THE NEED FOR SPEED

It is of no use to search for those facts and understandings which cause war and delay peace unless they can be found in time. Our questions must be answered soon or not at all.

Back of what the writers have to say in this chapter are four simple assumptions. In the first place, the hour *is* late (later than most people seem to think, judging by the irrelevance of their behaviour). Secondly, there is no reliable method faster than the scientific. Thirdly, this lateness of the hour is a most compelling argument for striving scientifically for peace know-how without delay and in the most rapid fashion practicable. Fourthly, the scientific process, like any other human process, can be speeded up. These assumptions and their implications become more explicit in the next few pages.

Ours is a fast age. It is getting faster. Our days are dangerous and dizzy. The movement of our culture, as well as that of individuals, is rapid. Not only is there high speed to our cars and trains and planes, but these speeds accelerate. Decade by decade, new instruments or tools for doing things and getting places drive slower ones off the market. Nor do we move slowly politically. Continually, for better or for worse, new alliances or mergers take place in relatively short time. Historians talk of thirty-year wars. Mid-twentieth century strategists talk of wars of thirty hours. Not only may wars become shorter. They may come more shortly.

If we are to discover the know-how for peace and survival, it must be discovered before the date of doom by atomic fire. The race between Atomic Doom Date and Peace Know-how Date is crucial. This chapter is written under the assumption that no one can predict precisely the date of World War III, nor with accuracy its finality. The longer its postponement, the more complete its destruction (if it come). Ordinarily the question: Is there time? can be answered by answering two other questions: How much time is there? and How much time is required? To neither of these is there a definite answer.

How much time do we have? The late Justice Rutledge of the U.S. Supreme Court was asked in 1948 by the writer, 'Do we have time?' His deliberate reply was, 'You have all the time there is.' This is an heroic answer. Courage and intelligence demand that we make high use of time 'while time remains'.

To assume that there is no time at all is as fatal as to assume that time is unlimited. In case there is time, let us not be guilty of having refused to use it. We have everything to gain if we win. We have nothing to lose by trying. Whatever time there is, it is not getting greater, at least not through inaction. It is shorter today than yesterday. It will be shorter tomorrow than today, if we fail to act.

The time required is a function of (*a*) the size of the job, and (*b*) the speed with which we work. How much knowledge will we have to acquire, how much research effort will it take, to discover the know-how for peace? Overestimation or underestimation is a liability only insofar as it unfavourably affects our incentive and our effort. On the one hand, we have people who seem to assume that we already know all we need to know to achieve peace. On the other hand, there are great numbers who seem to feel that the problem is so great that no amount of honest intellectual effort could possibly crack it. The amount of work required to develop the first atomic bomb has been estimated at a million man-years of work. For our goal of peace the requirement may turn out to be the same or one-tenth as much or ten times as much. Whatever the size of the job, we must accept it or perish.

Whatever the facts about the size of the job, our real control over the length of time required is through attending to our second question: How fast will we work? If and as we are truly concerned about the time available and the time required, we will more and more turn our attention to the question of speed. Only by increasing the speed of our search for peace know-how can we decrease the time required. Only by decreasing the time required can we increase our chances of arriving on time with the knowledge necessary for survival.

In a practical sense, then, the question, Is there time? becomes, How can we achieve speed? This is our paramount question. To answer this, we must inquire into the nature of scientific speed.

The Need for Men

Now any scientific development consists of a series of events or discoveries. The shorter the time interval between discoveries, the faster the development. If the time lapse between events can be shortened, the process can be speeded up. A further observation is that speed of development is positively correlated with stage of development. The further a science has gone, the faster it goes. Somewhat as with the speed of a falling body, there is a striking tendency toward acceleration. As is often pointed out, more scientific progress has occurred in the last 500 years than in the previous 5,000, and more in the last fifty years than in the previous 500.

Just how does stage of development function in acceleration in science? Let us look particularly at two objective features in the general concept of stage of development. One of the most obvious features is that of the amount of information collected. The more facts that have been discovered and explained by comprehensive theory, the further we say the science has progressed. Facts discovered and theories developed may be considered as tools. A fact or theory can be a tool with which to think and with which to get more facts. Consider some of the more common facts we now possess in the realm of human physiology. The blood circulates;

the red corpuscles carry oxygen, and white corpuscles fight disease; the heart pumps the blood; the oxidation of certain materials is required for the building of cells; air is necessary for oxidation; lungs in the process of respiration are necesary for oxidation; etc., etc. Hippocrates and his fellow members in the Athenian Medical Association had no such array of facts in their tool kit. With these knowledges in their possession, medical scientists have gone on to discover further factors in the physiological process, such as enzymes, vitamins, endocrine glands and their hormones. With these, they are expected to make much greater progress in the prevention of disease and the postponement of death.

Highly related to this factor of increased information is the factor of improved techniques and instruments for gaining more knowledge. The role played by these instruments and methods in so-called natural science has been referred to in previous chapters. Some techniques and instruments for the aid of social science are such instruments as the I.Q. Tests, the Rorschach Ink Blot Test, the Thematic Apperception Test, and such techniques as: attitude opinionaires, personality inventories, depth interviewing, open-ended questions, and various other procedures in opinion and attitude research. All these make great contribution to the dynamics of scientific method. Leeuwenhoek, inventor of the microscope, perhaps never dreamed of a microscope that would magnify ten thousand times. It is not unlikely that some day social scientists will have instruments for social measurement and observation ten, twenty or fifty times as revealing as the ones they now use.

But there are subjective features which are highly important. The factors of increased information, improved observation, and better method have a profoundly invigorating effect on that indispensable factor in all science, known as curiosity. Our curiosity is challenged by what we already know, by what we see, and by our facility for getting at further knowledge. These achievements not only make us more able but also more willing to further explore and discover. It is often said that science raises more questions than it answers.

Highly related to this factor of curiosity is another subjective factor—confidence. Success leads to success partly because success leads to confidence and confidence leads to further success. This was doubtless in the mind of E. L. Thorndike when he stated that the mother of invention is not necessity but previous invention. Science depends in part upon our confidence in science, which, in a sense, amounts to confidence in intelligence.

These subjective factors of curiosity and confidence would seem to exert a marked effect upon our factor of manpower; i.e., the number of scientific people on the job. This we wish to stress as a further objective feature in the stage of development of a science. Let us make a two-way comparison of modern chemistry with (a) a previous stage of chemistry, and (b) a less rapid science, social psychology.

Chemistry's progress today compared with that of fifty years ago is amazing. The number of members in the American Chemical Society in 1900 was 1,715. As of 1950, it was 63,000. Both chemists and psychologists generally would admit that chemistry today is moving at a much higher speed than is psychology, especially social psychology. According to one recent survey, the number of members of the American Psychological Association was about 7,000. Psychologists whose major interest is social psychology represent about five per cent of this total, about 350 persons. If we add to this number 150 social psychologists listed in other scientific societies, such as the American Sociological Society, we would have 50,000 chemists to 500 social psychologists—a ratio of 100 to 1. These figures illustrate the idea which we are trying to present, that the speed of development in a science is correlated with the number of scientific workers in that area.

At the risk of certain dangers from oversimplification, may we now suggest that we have a cycle consisting of three major features: (a) scientific knowledge developed; (b) scientific morale; and (c) scientific manpower. In this cycle, increases in (a) lead to increases in (b), which lead to increases in (c), which lead to increases in (a); etc., etc. Affect any one of these and you affect the others in turn.

Now let us raise the question, Where in this cycle can human decision lay hold? Of these factors which control the speed of science, which one can we deliberately control? The inescapable answer is: *the number of the workers*. The greater the number of scientific workers engaged, the greater the number of scientific events or discoveries made in a given period of time. To illustrate with hypothetical numbers, let us assume that a highly fruitful point in the development of a science of peace is reached after 100 highly significant discoveries take place. If these discoveries average one per year, the total process will take 100 years. If they average ten per year, it might take only ten years. Discoveries in science are not so accidental as is sometimes supposed. To quote from David Bradley:

Dr. Teller, a great scientist who reluctantly continued working at Los Alamos, after the war, has written: 'If atom bombs lead to disaster, it will not be by accidental catastrophe, but careful planning and design.' Dr. Teller might have added that if atomic energy is to lead to peace and plenty, it will also not be by accident but by careful planning and design.

We cannot go out and buy ready-made the knowledge in terms of either fact or instrument or method. But we can employ specialists to do so, here as well as in weaponeering. As to curiosity, we cannot manufacture it, but we can cultivate it and we can release it where it exists. A great many months of discussion with both scientists and laymen convinces us that there is much more desire for and curiosity about peace than is now operative. This interest and potential interest has its own restrictive blocks. It is our business to uncover and remove these restrictions.

Men Available

Granted that we men of earth need peace as nothing else, still we do not know how to get it. We have said that by science we can find out—by enough of us going to work at it, we can speed up the science of peace and thus greatly increase the probability of our survival. Now a further question is, If the psychological and economic restrictions are removed, are there enough scientific workers available? Do suitable persons exist? Let us roughly examine the data.

There are two billion human beings on this planet. If we limit ourselves to the adult working-age population, this figure might be cut to one billion. If the need is for a million scientific workers, this represents not more than one worker out of every thousand. If war elimination is our number one job, we might well afford to operate all other causes on 99·9 per cent of our manpower. We *can* spare enough workers for the purpose of a peace science.

But how many of the billion adult and active members of the

human society are suitable for the kind of work that we have in mind when we propose a science of peace? A scientific enterprise utilizes a wide variety and a wide range of talent. Not only are research teams to be made up of experts of a good many different kinds, but they may also include a great many people who would not think of themselves as highly expert: clerical workers, statistical clerks, maintenance workers, etc.

To illustrate, let us again refer to the Manhattan Project in the U.S.A. for developing the atomic bomb. It has been estimated that 250,000 people worked on this project. Now Vanevar Bush has estimated that the total number of U.S.A. scientists during World War II under the registry of the Office of Scientific Research and Development, over which he presided, was over 35,000. Even if as many as 25,000 of these worked on the atomic bomb project, we would have a ratio of one scientist out of no less than every ten workers.

Further, if we could count the number of key scientists, such as Fermi, Szilard, Oppenheimer, Urey, Bohr, etc., perhaps the number 25 might account for much of the talent at that level. We could then extend our estimate to say that, for every top scientist, we need 1,000 scientists and 9,000 or 10,000 other workers.

It is a fact that occupational groups do expand. Automobile mechanics have expanded from practically nothing in the U.S.A. at the beginning of the twentieth century to something like half a million in 1950. Railway workers have grown from almost nothing in 1850 to one million a century later. The number of Ph.D. degrees granted by universities has increased markedly in the last 50 years. Such expansions take place only under favourable conditions. The recent rapid expansion of the number of clinical psychologists in the U.S.A. is a case in point. Largely as a part of the U.S. veterans' programme with a very liberal policy of training, the number of clinical psychologists expanded greatly in the first five years after the end of World War II. The newest division of the American Psychological Association is the division of military psychology. Doubtless the largest employer of psychologists in the U.S. is the Department of Defense. This was not true fifteen years ago.

Much of this rapid expansion in occupational rosters has taken place by transfers. One occupation gives place to another according to practical demand. Men who would once have become blacksmiths now become motor-car mechanics. The scientists engaged in the rapidly developed atomic bomb project were not all newly-become scientists. Many were drawn from existing projects and activities. They were quickly drawn because of the priority given by one nation to the job of winning a war. Is it not conceivable that a priority can be given to the job of winning peace?

Primarily, this urgently required transfer means a change in the goal of the workers involved. It means a shift from serving the needs of individual nations for power and position to serving the needs of all mankind for increased human harmony. These transfers, however, include some modification of ability. Any scientific programme will give serious concern to the development of appropriate competence. Millions of dollars are spent annually by industry on apprentices in various fields of physical and commercial research. National governments are increasingly providing training for the young scientists who are expected to carry on their programmes of armament research. Any effective programme for scientific research on peace must concern itself with the preparation of its scientists.

To the question, then, Are suitable men available? our answer is, Yes, if we are willing to take men who are potentially suitable and to furnish the conditions favourable to their development. But where are these potentially suitable persons? What are they doing now? How are they now classified?

The first group is that of social scientists, men who are now doing research in human relations of one sort or another, and who are schooled in the ideology or theory of social research. These might be represented by a figure of less than 100,000 persons. In 1946, Robert W. Leeper estimated that for the U.S.A. alone, the social scientists numbered 25,000. From among these might come the people who would require the least re-training or re-orientation time to be ready for topmost planning and for creative as well as more technical routine work.

A second group of individuals would be those who would not necessarily call themselves scientists, but who are highly experienced in the observation and interpretation of human relations. These include journalists, clergymen, educators, public relations workers, market research technicians, salesmen, advertisers, and others.

A third group is that of physical scientists. There are some who believe that the skill and the training received in the physical sciences would make this group eventually more potent in social science than even the first group mentioned. It is assumed that under appropriate circumstances many physical scientists would be willing to redirect their scientific drive in the direction of better human relations, particularly toward peace at this time. The number here to be drawn from is several hundred thousand.

A fourth group is composed of current students and recent graduates from colleges and universities the world over. These would come from:

    1. those who have a present hope or desire for spending their lives in social science;

    2. those who, for certain reasons, have been looking forward to physical science, but who would prefer, under more favourable conditions, to work on problems of human relations;

    3. those who have been preparing for other vocations or who have not made up their minds.

This is undoubtedly one of our largest groups, but will probably require a longer time for the necessary learning. We cannot tell to what extent this will be offset by the lack of necessity to unlearn many things with which the older groups may be handicapped.

Fifth, there are other individuals, who have never seen the inside of a college, but who, by virtue of certain special abilities, or high general ability, or special temperament, would be well suited for peace science work, granted a reasonable amount of training and experience. It is here assumed that a Ph.D. degree is not an infallible token of research qualification, nor is an A.B. The size of this group is hard to envision. Similar to these is a group of skilled people from which would be supplied the greater percentage of our million—individuals whose requirements for successful contribution are more or less technical. We refer to clerical workers and mechanical workers of certain types. If we are right in our assumption that the problem is in the minds of men, and that the way to find out is to ask people, we will need a great many interviewers, a job for which millions might qualify.

But are enough of these persons willing? Here again, the real answer can come best by trial. Preliminary research might throw light on this. We wish to report two very small studies:

    1. In a small sample of social scientists of the Middle West, U.S.A., who responded to a questionnaire, 32 per cent indicated

that they would be willing to work full-time, in their professional capacities, on a project for peace, even if the salary were 20 per cent less than they are at present getting.

2. College students, when asked if they would be willing to enrol in a peace college if one were available, answered thus: 27 per cent would surely enrol; 25 per cent would most likely enrol.

We believe that the fundamental working proposition might be as follows: There are many more men now able and willing than are working at the science of peace, and there are many more men capable and willing to be trained than are now being trained. Our business is to bring about the conditions for employment and training of the 'unemployed' and the 'untrained'.

This chapter has dealt with the need for speed, the means of getting it, and the availability of the means. Since time is short and cannot be lengthened, and the distance is great and cannot be shortened, the only thing we can do anything about is the speed with which we travel. The only way we have of affecting this speed is through the number of us who choose and are chosen to go to work at it. The number of us who could be spared to work on this problem, even though it be but a fraction of 1 per cent of the total of the human family, can amount to one or more million workers.

10
MANPOWER THROUGH MONEY POWER

> Even though genius cannot be bought, many a genius has defaulted because he had to eat.
> HERBERT HOOVER

> Shall we put our faith in science or in something else? ... This is the question. ... If it is answered in the affirmative, then social research institutions will make their appearance which will rank with Massachusetts and California Institutes of Technology, Mellon Institute, the research laboratories of Bell Telephone, General Electric and General Motors, not to mention some 2000 others.
> GEORGE LUNDBERG

> This is the gamble, then, that our Nation might take. It would not require that we abandon any other mode of approach which we think also looks promising. It would not be impossibly costly. In fact, compared with the expenditures on unemployment relief, on modern prisons, on battleships, or on military training, the cost of a vastly expanded programme of social science would be absurdly small.
> ROBERT LEEPER

At various points in our previous chapters we have intimated that the proposal for peace through science includes the appropriation of the money necessary for its development. In this chapter we wish to discuss this matter of financing peace research as a distinct problem. In the preceding chapter we have attempted to make clear the indispensable role of manpower. In this chapter we wish to emphasize the role of money power.

A science of peace, if it comes, will come, like all other major social events, not as a single isolated happening, but as a series of inter-related events, involving a number of interacting factors. If we leave out a single factor essential to the total process, the process will fail to proceed.

The elemental and fundamental importance of finance in the process of peace research is in its relation to the release of manpower. We have suggested that a million scientific workers fulltime may be necessary to exhaust the possibilities of a scientific approach to peace. We have suggested that these workers can be made available. But note this most challenging fact: these workers are not now on the job. Indispensable to their going to work is financial arrangement for wages or salary to make possible subsistence while they are on the job. Full personal attention to the problem of peace requires freedom from conflicting demands. As long as we consider peace or peace research a task which requires small effort and small skill, the importance of financing is not apparent. But if achieving peace know-how is a job calling for the utmost use of intelligence by a large number of intellectually skilled people, the necessity for money to finance their employment is immediately obvious. Utmost service requires minimal pay. This in turn requires adequate budget.

It is believed by some that there are other aspects of the problem which are more important, and that if these are solved, the problem of financing will take care of itself. This we believe to be a fatal assumption. The financial problem is not the last to be solved. It is one of the first. We live under an economy in which men seldom work without wages. Obviously, we require the dollars to set the date at which persons go to work. This includes work at the preliminary and exploratory stages.

Two or three persons who have read a preliminary draft of this chapter appeared to have been shocked that a matter so crass and 'secular' as money should be bluntly mentioned in connection with a matter so idealistic and 'sacred' as peace.

We have not found it feasible to relieve the hard facts of their bluntness. Peace research means work. Work means wages. Wages means money. The failure to embrace this principle we believe is responsible for the relatively low level of peace search throughout our world. Seldom do we find a person exclusively employed to search for peace.

No sizeable work programme in the world operates without a significant budget. Paid personnel operate our hospitals, schools and courts. To assume that we must pay doctors to dispense medicine, teachers to dispense wisdom, judges to dispense justice, while overlooking the need to pay people to devote their best energies to peace, is fallacious and fatal. Real salaries are paid for research workers where the goal is a more deadly weapon. We dare not ignore the need for salaries for scientific search for peace!

We have said that money is indispensable. But what a dilemma! Money for peace, and especially for peace research, is hard to come by. The financial problem is truly a problem. To underestimate it is to fail to solve it. Its difficulty is as great as the difficulty of changing our habits of spending and our thinking about spending. If we examine the private and public budgets of men and of nations the world over, we find them full of a great variety of million- and billion-dollar items, but none of these is labelled *peace*. No government in the world appropriates a dollar to a department of peace. Yet departments of defence are deluged with dollars. The Department of Defense in the U.S.A., to use one illustration, in order to provide for the training and employment of upwards of 10 million persons in schools, camps and factories, in 1952 had a budget of over 50 billion dollars. This averages over 333 dollars per man, woman and child in the nation. Is this normal? Yesterday—no. Tomorrow—yes, unless we use 'real' money to make it possible for men to use 'real' intelligence to find a *real* solution to the problem of international conflict.

So much for the indispensability and the difficulty of finding a solution to the problem of financing peace research. Surely this problem must have a solution. We have great economic and psychological potential. Our world's economic power is extensive and under appropriate circumstances highly flexible. The basic motives of men are preponderantly for ends to which peace is indispensable. Much money now circulates, and flows in many directions. What greater use have we for a million or a billion dollars? The appropriations we have made for other social ends —health, education, justice—indicate the immensity of our possibilities. Our economy is not bankrupt—nor is our goodwill.

Let us now address ourselves to the question, Where is the money coming from? To this question we cannot give complete and specific answers at this time. But let us attempt some partial and general ones. Where does the money come from for other social arrangements for making division of labour operate? Primarily, of course, the source is the people, all people, great masses of people the world over who support directly or indirectly the institutions by which they live. But there must exist agencies through which this money is channelled into specific projects aimed toward specific goals.

There are many instances where large numbers of individuals have combined their financial contributions for the furtherance of a single goal. At a local level, we have, in most large cities in the U.S.A., annual Community Chest Drives. On a national scale, there are such agencies as the American Red Cross, the National Association for the Advancement of Coloured People, the National Foundation for Infantile Paralysis, the American Heart Association. Some of these number their contributing members in the hundreds of thousands.

However, if we want to illustrate social expenditure on a vast scale we have to turn to government. A very large percentage of the average citizen's dollar goes to pay local, regional or national taxes. At the city or county level, we combine our financial resources to support for mutual benefit such services as municipal waterworks, garbage disposal, fire and police protection, public schools and care of streets and parks. States and provinces provide further services, but the biggest agencies for the spending of money for public works and general welfare in the world today are national governments. A project such as the Tennessee Valley Authority in the U.S.A., or the Damodar Valley Project in India is beyond the financial level of any private individual or philanthropic organization or even a single industrial corporation. The postal service in every country is a governmental function. Responsibility for roads and highways is shared by national, regional, and local governments; but the expanding network of super-highways over a country is largely a result of national aid and planning. Increasingly education has come to require resources greater than that of private individuals or organizations. It is becoming increasingly felt that anything short of national financial aid is inadequate. The welfare state is the national state.

The adequacy of national government is measured by the degree to which it makes possible those services most needed by its citizens. It is sometimes true that national governments support activities designed to benefit the general welfare, not only of their own citizens, but of people in other parts of the world. Perhaps the appropriations of the various nations for the support of U N and its specialized agencies, though regrettably small, are among the best examples of national 'world-mindedness' thus far. However, it should be noted that national governments are not likely to act to benefit citizens of other nations unless they conceive this action as necessary to the welfare of their own citizens. More enlightened self-interest at the national level is one of our better hopes.

Also, governments often seem not very forward-looking in the field of social welfare. Too seldom do government officials anticipate a need and provide for it before it becomes acute. For instance, the measures taken during the thirties in the U.S.A. to alleviate suffering caused by the depression were set up only after the need for them had become so acute as to precipitate a crisis. Nothing adequate in the way of preventive economic medicine was administered during the twenties. It was a long time from the deterioriation of the first 'blighted' areas in U.S. cities to the opening of the first governmentally sponsored housing project. This same tardiness of social conscience can be seen in the record of other nations at various times. Nations differ here but it is only a matter of time and degree.

Further, it often happens that non-governmental agencies must pioneer and demonstrate a means of attacking a particular problem, as well as develop public sensitivity to the problem, before government officials will act upon the problems. Many of the various social welfare activities—employment agencies, child welfare, care of the aged, etc.—now considered governmental functions in many countries were first initiated, supported and lobbied for by private philanthropy. This feature could prove a serious or even fatal handicap where speed is so essential as in the case of finding the preventive for hydrogen war.

To summarize briefly, then, it would seem that there are three facts which must be taken into account in any consideration of the financing of a science of peace. First, it would seem that no institution smaller than a national government has the resources for such financing. Second, official leaders of a national government tend to have too limited a sense of global responsibility to motivate action for global welfare. Third, such a government is not very likely (judging by past records) to act in a pioneering fashion. Although it may sometimes be true that a government will lead the large majority of its people by a particular action, it also is true that the government in this action is following a trail blazed by a few pioneers. Often the governmental leader seems to be following the crowd.

But the science of peace which we have been describing is international in scope. It should be designed to work with and to benefit peoples of all lands. Thus it is with national governments in their role of financial supporters of international organizations that we are primarily concerned. Such financing will be undertaken by national governments as there is sufficient growth in the belief that the best interests of a particular nation's citizens will be furthered by furthering the interests of people the world over. This will happen regarding peace as we become more and more aware of how *indispensable* and how *indivisible* peace is. At this present stage our national governments probably cannot be counted upon to pioneer, but will more likely act on the stimulus of exploratory or preliminary activities carried on by nongovernmental agencies designed to promote the belief that science is a feasible method for dealing with the problem of war elimination and the building of peace.

How can adequate scientific action on behalf of peace, on the part of national governments, be brought about? Let us take up the three levels of action—international, national, and nongovernmental—and see how they might operate.

An International Organization

A logical organization through which the financing for a science of peace would come would be the United Nations, since it is an organization already in existence, with machinery for sponsoring agencies to perform specialized jobs, such as UNESCO, WHO, ILO, ITO, FAO, etc., and financially supported by the majority of national governments in the world. The UN is imperfect, of course, but it exists as a mechanism for global welfare, and this is a strong point in its favour. It is possible for it to be changed, strengthened, improved, adapted to the jobs it must perform.

UNESCO is probably the agency which comes the closest in spirit to our ideal of an agency for an international science of peace. Its total appropriations are unbelievably small, but it is a precedent for global scientific service financed through national governments. Qualitatively it is an excellent illustration of international intellectual co-operation.

We have here a principle and a precedent that can be extended a thousandfold, providing popular sentiment can be developed, identified and brought to bear. The fact that present international government is not situated as yet to levy tribute directly upon its people leads us to our emphasis upon our next classification.

National Governments

Sixty or more national governments in the world are now giving the United Nations and its specialized agencies varying degrees of financial and moral support. Thus precedent has been established and continues for national support of international co-operation on such vital matters as food, health, communication, trade, education, labour, banking, aviation and postal service. These services could surely be justified on the basis of both humanitarianism and enlightened self-interest. To these UN specialized agencies could very readily be added an agency for the support and co-ordination of a science of peace, if the member nations felt such action to be to their self-interest. To help the nations develop readiness for co-operative scientific search for international harmony is the greatest opportunity and challenge awaiting our next group of agencies.

Non-Governmental Organizations

The role of pioneering for peace research is open to any existing group or organization with breadth and flexibility of purpose and interest sufficient to commission full-time workers. For any one organization the number need not be large. It could well be at the outset, anywhere from one to a thousand workers. The value of these early exploratory activities might in part be promotional and in part more purely scientific. Even if strictly scientific their eventual function could well be to prime the larger pump at the national treasuries. As an example, a small organization might provide for a conference, lasting from three days to three months, of leading social scientists to work out a preliminary plan for concrete, specific action, either governmental or non-governmental, on a science of peace. A larger organization might set up a permanent full-time commission of 5 or 50 experts for the same purpose. Exploratory surveys of opinion on questions closely related to the problem of financing peace research might be conducted. There are endless possibilities here. Some of these have been suggested in previous chapters dealing with the nature of a science of peace.

There are several types of existing organizations through which such activity could be financed and co-ordinated. Let us list some of these:

A. FOUNDATIONS

According to the Russell Sage Foundation in reporting a recent survey of philanthropic, privately organized foundations, there are about 505 of these in the U.S.A. Of these, it has been estimated that, judging by their stated aims and purposes of organization, 45 might be interested in a project of a social scientific nature. Of these, only a few are well known. The Rockefeller Foundation, the Carnegie Foundation, the Carnegie Endowment for International Peace, and the Ford Foundation are among the most familiar.

It may be well here to sound a note of caution concerning foundations in general. There is an unfortunate tendency for the ordinary citizen to turn too quickly to foundations as the first and ultimate source of scientific 'charity'. Foundations are in no position to carry the whole load in any wide social enterprise. They have distinct qualitative as well as quantitative limits. For instance, they have been accused recently, and with considerable justice, by Edwin Embree, of 'timidity'. They are no longer pioneers, trail-blazing in the wilderness of social problems and urgent human needs. They prefer to stay on the settled fringes, supporting activities which should long ago have been taken over by state and national governments. They are often cautious, preferring to support lines of research that are already well established, rather than support pioneer research. In their conservatism they have been governed by the kind of knowledge and techniques we already have rather than by obvious need for new methods and for knowledge in new directions. Risk capital is fully as essential in scientific enterprise as elsewhere.

However, despite certain depressing aspects of foundation support, we would stress two points: (*a*) they have acted as social trail-blazers in the past, with courage and imagination; and (*b*) they represent a very considerable amount of wealth, which, however indirectly, is yet popular wealth, derived from the labour of the people, and from the fruits of their earth. The 505 foundations mentioned above have a total capital of $1,800,000,000. They represent a possible source of financial support which must not be overlooked. Moreover, they have in the past in many instances transcended national boundaries in their sympathies and expenditures. Then too there is always the possibility that an old foundation might be converted or a new one set up for the exclusive purpose of getting our greatest method (science) applied to our greatest problem (peace). No foundation (to the writer's knowledge) has as yet said courageously, decisively and positively, and with their dollars, that mankind is devoid of the necessary know-how for peace.

B. UNIVERSITIES

The universities are institutions suited for the channelling of wealth toward the support of sustained intellectual activity. The university campus is the scene of a great number of research projects today. Many universities and many individuals, by virtue of their professional connection with universities, are the recipients of foundation and governmental appropriations for research. Unfortunately, here as in other instances, there is a disproportion between physical and social science appropriations. Where there is concern with human relations, there is much academic dialecticism and a dearth of objective research. However, there are on university campuses encouraging examples of social science activity, such as: The Laboratory of Social Relations and The Institute of Creative Altruism at Harvard, the Human Development Laboratory at the University of Chicago, and Washington Public Opinion Laboratory at the University of Washington, to mention only a few in one nation.

No other set of institutions has so great a responsibility for guiding the intelligence of youth towards problems of greatest significance. The university has been well defined as 'the intellectual focus of those activities which contribute to the welfare of mankind.' World-oriented universities could be a great step towards our ideal world community. We cannot wait too long to have intelligence focused on peace.

C. SEMI-COMMERCIAL RESEARCH AGENCIES

These are less important than either foundations or universities in the amount of money which they have available for non-commercial, non-partisan research projects. There have been, however, a few instances of agencies which set aside a certain part of their profits from commercial research to initiate socially desirable projects for which there was no commercial sponsor. Two agencies of this type are the National Opinion Research Center at Chicago, and the Survey Research Center at Ann Arbor, Michigan. These non-profit organizations, so meagrely supported philanthropically as to require contracts from special interests to keep afloat, are among the least commercial of a large number of organizations now exploring the U.S. public mind. With only a few millions of free dollars they could do a superb job of helping us all find out what we all need to know about what we all want.

D. OTHER AND SPECIAL ORGANIZATIONS FOR PEACE

Instances of social scientific research support coming from non-commercial organizations or individual sources yet unmentioned are rare, but not totally lacking. Church groups, labour unions, consumer co-operatives, world government organizations, and professional associations do occasionally sponsor research on problems with which they are confronted. Only one of the reasons for paucity of research here is the lack of money with which to finance it. Another reason is often lack of interest in the scientific approach. Some religious groups, however, are notably interested in peace, and where their views are not inharmonious with the use of the scientific method, there is ground for hope for co-operation.

The general rule, however, is that present-day organizations, whether religious, fraternal, social, political, professional, business or labour, are set up for purposes other than peace. Very, very few exist for peace *per se*; practically none for a science of peace. This is tragic. Whether considered as a scientific or as a political job, international peace requires co-operation. For effective action individuals require organization through which to co-operate. If the present organizations do not offer adequate media for action the alternative is new organization. This however anticipates the theme of the next chapter.

An example of a small group organized and maintained primarily for promoting peace research is the Character Research Association which has sponsored the writing of this book. Incorporated in 1945, it consists of a small number of laymen who pool their moral influence and contribute from $10 to $100 per year to the common fund. Without any great change in their way of life the members thus make it possible for one or more persons to devote full time serving the paramount value of peace through science.

Summary

In this chapter we have dealt with the problem of finding the money with which to release the manpower for a science of peace. We have emphasized that men are not likely to work for peace at the levels required by science unless they are paid. Peace wages are as essential for waging peace as war wages for waging war. We have indicated that our economic practices and our monetary attitudes have to be modified if a peace-science budget is to materialize. However, the economic and the psychic resources are abundantly potentially available. All we need is an adequate orientation. To get at the nature of this orientation, we have discussed the possible sources for the necessary funds. By the nature of the problem, funds should be administered by an international organization, and the source should be global. The biggest source of big money, however, is big government. Hence we turn to the hope that national governments will make the appropriations out of a sense of the need for the security and welfare of their own citizens and increasingly out of a sense of the economic and moral oneness of mankind. The necessary stimulation can be produced by non-governmental organizations which demonstrate the feasability of the problem's solution and otherwise prime the pumps for greater flow of 'bigger' dollars.

Whether we think of governments international or national, or of organizations governmental or non-governmental, all action waits on the decision and the motivation of individual men. We are challenged with the threat of extinction. For the solution of this unsolved problem we have a method suitable and adaptable. We have the manpower available. To release this manpower would require a fraction of one per cent of our present flow of money. What we lack is the decision—the decision to spend the money to hire the men to apply the method to solve the problem. This decision will have to grow out of some sentiment. This sentiment constitutes our problem. How to find it, how to mobilize it, and how to develop it, will be the subject of the next chapter.

11

INDIVIDUAL AND GROUP ACTION

> Maturity is harder than childhood. Responsibility and realism involve terrific costs. They mean taking up a burden which one could easily avoid, thinking when one might so easily follow, taking the chance of being wrong when one might so easily appear always right, incurring the opprobrium of being a busybody. Indeed, the cost of being socially and politically mature is so great that few have been willing to pay it.
>
> GARDNER MURPHY

WAR is perpetuated *by people*. War must be eliminated *by people*. War elimination must be initiated and consummated by people. The scientific beginnings of this process can be initiated and promoted only as individual men and women *act* and *act co-operatively*. The nexus of our problem is this relation between individual decision and collective action. Our problem is how to build the bridge from our unorganized present to a speedily organized tomorrow. This twofold requirement of individual decision for co-operative action throws a great strain upon our human faith—our social confidence. It calls for belief in the possibility of 'a million individuals' supporting this scientific movement when no more than ten or two or one is at hand.

With this in mind let us envision a grass-roots movement, starting with each of a 'million' persons. We will sketch this in only six tentative preliminary steps. Our outline should be considered as a sort of model, useful for illustrating some of the principles needed in any vital process in which the reader is likely to participate.

STEP 1. MAKE A DATE WITH ONESELF

Perhaps the very first of the worthwhile steps is to make a date with oneself for purposes of coming to a decision regarding one's intended expenditures or efforts. Having discussed this problem with a great many people, we are impressed that the first and foremost cause of inaction in this connection is due to failure to take time for those considerations which are necessary for an earnest and valid formulation of intention. If the road to atomic hell is paved with good intentions, it is because the intentions are not good enough. For all defects of intention there is a cure, but it comes at a cost. The cost is patient and careful thought based upon a minimal amount of information regarding oneself, and the task at hand. So we repeat that the foremost requirement is a period of careful consideration.

This step is fraught with two opposite hazards, namely, indecision and decision premature. Does one have enough information? Can he afford to wait while hunting vigorously for more information? It is highly crucial that he come to some kind of decision, progressively and soon. Our impression is that the cause of peace in general, and of peace research and peace research financing in particular, suffers not so much from wrong decision as from indecision. Faith without works is dead. Thought without decision is stultifying. This brings us to our second suggestion.

STEP 2. MAKE AN INDIVIDUAL APPROPRIATION

The individual should make an appropriation calling for the expenditure of a realistic amount of his money and of his time. We would like to discuss first the necessity for a personal financial appropriation. There may be on the part of some a treacherous temptation to put off the moment of financial decision. Some of us may easily find ourselves in the position where we are thinking first about the other person's money and later, if at all, about our own, instead of the other way around. Eventually we must commit ourselves to the proposition that in research and research promotion 'it is money that makes the mare go'. It is exceedingly important that this decision on money be stated in some definite terms.

What is said about money is equally true about time. It is often assumed, and we think fallaciously, that it is easier to get people to contribute valuable time than it is to get them to contribute value in the form of dollars. What we may be observing is that it is easier to get them to *promise* their time than their dollars. We have found over a long period of time that time promises are much less clear and reliable than dollar promises. In regard to both time and money, we think there is a very vital psychological factor in the making of the appropriation in definite and calculable terms.

Perhaps no other factor would do more to lift the cause of peace and peace research from its present exceedingly low psychological level. No one would expect to run a bank or a railway or a school with the services of individuals who would say that they would help, but whose indication did not enable one to tell when the individual would report for work nor how long he would stay on the job. Nor would one think of launching on an enterprise requiring money unless and except as individuals indicated definnite amounts. The financial capitalization of a programme of peace research must be taken as seriously as the capitalization of any other social enterprise.

STEP 3. CONTACT OTHER INDIVIDUALS

Isolation is fatal to co-operation. The concerned individual who has appropriated time can probably make no better use of this time than to use it to find prospective co-operators. If he has appropriated money he needs to find other money—money of other people—to keep his money company. As we stated in Chapter 2, the strength of the individual is no match for the momentum of our culture. Only man in his collective stature is fit to master his social fate. Only dynamic association among individuals of insight, foresight, and courage can give us the initial and necessary intellectual, material, and moral capital.

We have found that this job of making contacts with other concerned individuals is fraught with enormous possibilities of frustration. We would like to add certain precautions. In the first place, it will be easier if the individual attempting to contact others has done an effective job at the two previous steps mentioned. Thinking the matter out for himself decisively and, hence, making an explicit appropriation of his own time and money, can make the meaning of his talk to others less vague and ambiguous. In the second place, he should be forewarned that the number of individuals who are seriously looking for a chance to co-operate, while very large in the absolute, may be, percentage-wise, very small. As one talks to every Tom, Dick and Harry he meets on the problem of financing peace research, he will use up an enormous amount of time. What is probably more fatal, he may find his own morale and his own courage weakened by a tremendous display of inertia and indifference, or at any rate, hesitation and indecision. One must be prepared to take in his stride a variety of such abortive and essentially irrelevant responses as the following: 'You have a very, very difficult problem.' 'You have a very noble purpose.' 'We hope you succeed.' 'You had better hurry, the international situation is very grave.' (Note the use of the second person pronoun instead of the first.) Hundreds of other distracting responses will be forthcoming, such as, blasts at 'the vile intentions' of the enemy state or 'the stupid or insincere tactics of the Minister of Foreign Affairs', besides a raft of comments on the rising delinquency rate, skulduggery in the market, infidelity in the family or hypocrisy in the Church. As a hazard to intercommunication in the attempt to discover prospective cooperators, one will experience many false alarms. Because of lack of insight or candour, many individuals will appear to be interested, but will not have made, nor be ready to make, the second step in our outline, that of appropriating a significant amount of their personal time and money. The problem which taxes one's skill to the utmost is to be able to identify the genuine article early in the process.

The most fatal fallacy of course, is to assume that because the first 'ten' persons interviewed appear indifferent there are therefore no concerned persons in the community. The need here is for a certain kind of advertising. Not only will our concerned individual be looking for other concerned individuals, but he should remember that someone is looking for him. He needs, therefore, to do what he can to make himself visible to others of like intent. Without intercommunication, mutual recognition is impossible.

STEP 4. FORM A GROUP OF INTERACTING INDIVIDUALS

With mutual recognition, this fourth step is natural, even inevitable. Particles of moisture in the air have qualities of attraction which result in the formation of drops of rain. Like-minded people have a natural mutual attraction that tends to take place as soon as their like-mindedness becomes apparent. The business of the individuals at this stage is to achieve quantity of association through repeated contact and deliberation.

This stage of the total process is one of pooling of various resources or assets. Doubtless the most indispensable and rare of all our assets is that of courage or morale. Only by achieving proximity and intercommunication can the pooling of attitudinal assets be achieved. Social or moral courage is no different in this respect from physical courage. The strength of the individual is in the pack. We have here not only a summating process, but a process of induction. We do not merely add the courage of separate individuals, but the courage of the separate individuals itself grows with cordial contact and with reciprocity of confidence.

Related to this process of strengthening of morale is the pooling of intellectual, social and material resources. What cannot be accomplished with the available, appropriate time of one individual might easily be accomplished with that of twenty (or twenty thousand) individuals. With the growth of morale and the increase of resources, the group becomes vigorous and dynamic, and evolutionary.

STEP 5. FORM A GROUP PLAN

Crucial to the evolution of the group is that of consolidating, strengthening, and implementing the group purpose through a practical plan. The plan will, of course, vary from group to group, because of differences in the group resources and the stage of its development. For instance, there is the factor of the size of the group. A highly promising and robust group might consist of only two persons. If these two persons are each willing to assume the financial burden of one-tenth of the wages of a full-time worker, their first and greatest consideration would be to find eight more similarly minded members or their equivalent.

Sooner or later, the plans of the group have to be related, not only to the amount of time and money the members are actually willing to invest, but their plans will have to take account of the kind of labour or activity to which the members are suited by talent or disposition. Doorbell-ringing may appeal to some; speech-making to others. Perusal of journals and newspapers and like sources would suit the taste of still others. In any event, if the group is to be sound and the group purpose robust, the plan or form which this purpose takes will have to grow in clarity and definiteness and be subject to change.

It is assumed in this chapter that the final hope for effectiveness is in the eventual cumulative impact of thousands of co-ordinated groups with a common scientific goal. In line with this, individual groups would ask constantly such questions as, What other groups are now active? What are they doing? How can we co-operate? How can we best contribute to our common goal? Can we help initiate other groups? Each group might conceive itself as the nucleus of a chapter of a potential Worldwide Society for the Promotion of a Science of Peace.

STEP 6. TAKE GROUP ACTION

Our question now becomes 'What can a group of individuals do? What are some of the things which might be done by a group whose members have achieved the strength and unanimity of purpose necessary for worth-while group action?'

In reading these suggestions one should not lose sight of the importance of how best to develop the strength of the group. Particularly we would make mention of the numerical and financial strength sufficient to command the services of one or more full-time workers. It might well be a constant effort of the group to pass the ball from the hands of volunteer to paid workers as soon as feasible. Any of the projects hereinafter listed would profit greatly from that regularity and quantity of labour which is exceedingly hard to get from volunteer workers. The writer has not been able to conceive of any important project where the services of full-time workers would not at least be highly desirable, if not indispensable.

Doubtless a great many kinds of activities will develop from the sincere deliberations within highly integrated groups. Neither our time nor vision enables us to present all these possibilities. All we can do here is to present *illustrative* case projects. We shall limit this to seven suggestions. In these illustrations we must not lose sight of the necessity to evolve increasing sentiment for support for peace research. In any educational or organizational or agitational project anticipated, we should keep keen the scientific edge or aspect of our problem. While our need is to develop a sense of need for scientific peace action, this may well be done in an atmosphere charged with the sense of need for peace action.

(a) A Peace Centre

In most communities, there is no well-advertised place to which an individual may turn if he has the impulse to do something for peace. The unleashing of our better impulses in favour of down-to-earth, effective action requires not only time on the part of the individual but also opportunity for action and a place to act. For peace action there is need for facilities comparable to what is available for carrying out our impulses in regard to other values. When one wishes to be convivial, there is the tavern; when one wishes to read, there is the library; for those who wish to worship, there is the church; for those who desire formal education, there is the state school or the university or other centre for adult education. For most people, there is no known place to which to turn because of this value called peace. There is need for a setting in which co-operation among the peace-minded can be facilitated, a place where each individual can go to advertise his peace intentions, scientific, financial, or otherwise.

Such a Peace Centre could be a common and regular meeting-place for various peace action groups, such as the Fellowship of Reconciliation, the Women's International League for Peace and Freedom, the United World Federalists, the Association for the United Nations, and such peace research organizations as might be organized. Even though some of these organizations be not primarily devoted to the scientific attack, their joint association could cultivate a peace-confident atmosphere. The pooling of problems might well engender a sense of need for research. Through such a centre, peace organizations which are too weak to maintain a separate office could co-operate and each pay part of the cost of a clerical staff. At such a place, there could be displayed at all times the literature of such organizations. Here might be conducted courses in international relations for those who feel the need to catch up on world events. It might be a place for seminars for specialists or semi-specialists, or a place for forums or debates on crucial issues, especially those related to essential questions of research methodology and research financing.

It could be a place where native individuals could meet persons from other lands. This place could function as a small library of books, pamphlets and periodicals devoted to special aspects of the cause of peace. Here could develop a roster of volunteer workers and a matching catalogue of necessary tasks. Such a centre might well function both to accommodate and service, and also to challenge and encourage the peace-minded. This proposal would seem to be valid for any community where there exist potentially active peace-concerned individuals.

(b) *A Community Survey*

This project might best be conceived as a systematic approach for finding other interested individuals. It would be a scientific and practical design to enable peace-concerned persons to become aware of each other. If we want to know about John Doe's interest in peace or peace research, one way to find out is to ask him. The survey could be conducted block by block, covering everyone within a given area. It could in part do for a very small segment of the population what is proposed for the whole world in Chapter 8. It could be the beginning of a far-reaching project in mental analysis. It might progressively reveal the explanation of popular inertia to the challenging menace of modern warfare. It might be the most practical project for any small group for increasing the numerical strength of their group. It might well be designed to measure levels of peace sentiment all the way from passive willingness to have peace, through interest in political action for peace, through sentiment for peace research, including desire to contribute financially. The writer and his colleagues have found in peace-sentiment surveys some of their most exciting and challenging experiences.

(c) *Surveys of Specialized Groups*

Packed away in the heads of various groups of specialists there is a large amount of knowledge from a wide variety of experience. Some of this might have significant relevance to our problem. Various groups of specialists of similar background and point of view might well become the object of different surveys. Such groups might be physical scientists, social scientists, political scientists, practical politicians, educational officials, etc. Apparently none of these groups have the answer. Any one of them, however, might furnish part of the answer if the sum total of the wisdom within the group were systematized or synthesized into a composite whole. One often wonders why the physical scientists, for instance, do not apply their scientific method to this problem of war which their discoveries have so terribly aggravated. Why do not the social scientists get together either to pool their intellectual capital to form a body of knowledge as a foundation for further thought and research, or to pool their moral influence to encourage political and financial support of an all-out scientific attack on the problem of war? Answers to these questions might in part be revealed by a careful survey of what the members of such specialized groups think. Such a survey, on a very limited sample of social scientists, was made by the Attitude Research Laboratory of St. Louis in 1949. The results were highly encouraging.

(d) A Clearing House for Peace Information

The need for intercommunication between scientific workers, between scientists and citizens, and between citizens and citizens is highly crucial. The Clearing House would attempt to facilitate to some slight degree the beginnings of an adequate intercommunicative process. There are continually little research experiments or projects being carried on in various schools and colleges throughout the world. The spreading of this information among the various scientifically minded, peace-concerned individuals is obviously needed. The various scientific disciplines have their journals. Surely there is a place for one devoted to the scientific discussion of the problem of peace.

The Research Exchange on the Prevention of War has made an excellent beginning towards this type of service, qualitatively speaking. Its scope is limited to exchange of ideas and information among scientists. This project was initiated by a small group of social psychologists and other social scientists in 1952. Their most successful activity has been the publication of a bi-monthly Bulletin under the editorship of A. I. Gladstone, of Swarthmore College, Swarthmore, Pennsylvania, U.S.A. Two other activities have been the holding of summer workshops and of scientific symposia in connection with scientific conventions. Thus far the participators have been almost entirely social scientists. Possibilities for participation by other concerned persons need to be explored.

Thus far the project has operated without funds and hence without full-time personnel. Both are greatly needed.

(e) A Peace Research Finance Commission

In Chapter 8 we emphasized the importance of the job of research planning. Even the job of planning an attack on the problem of financing the researchers, including the research planners, is a large order. In the early months of the atomic age, there was set up in the United States, what was sometimes called the Acheson-Lilienthal Atomic Control Committee, made up of highly skilled and relevantly informed individuals. This group of five men carried on in continuous session for nearly three months, gathering information from various specialists and looking at the problem from various angles. They came out of their sessions with what looked at the time, to many people, like a hopeful plan. The fact that the plan did not finally succeed of adoption should not discourage us from this kind of co-operative inquiry on the part of our best thinkers. This Acheson-Lilienthal group was commissioned to answer the question, 'How can we solve the problem of controlling atomic weapons?' We are here suggesting a group commissioned to face the question, 'How can we solve the problem of financing peace research?'

Ideally, such a commission should be made up of the most capable thinkers we can find, who are practical social psychologists conversant with the problem or problems involved in financing research of all sorts. A well-thought-out set of recommendations on the part of such a commission might go far in raising the morale of people in all levels of economic and intellectual power. It might motivate foundations and governments to make at least initial, if not comprehensive, attacks on the problem. Any small group resolved to see such a commission come into active operation would, of course, face the challenging job of finding the funds needed to operate the project.

(f) Promoting a Peace College

A much more ambitious objective of a group of concerned individuals would be establishment and maintenance of a Peace College. This project was described in Chapter 8. Here let us think of it as an experimental step on a very small scale. In an article entitled, 'Wanted—A West Point for Peace Leadership', Sylvanus Duvall said:

The trouble with the peace movements of the past has been that they have been led by amateurs who were, for the most part, exceedingly part-time.

The actual setting-up of a Peace College would mean the actual achievement of a division of labour for peace study. Here a small group of persons would be working, not part-time, but full-time and under circumstances favourable for rapidly outgrowing their amateur status. Such a college could consist of as few as ten or fifteen persons as an experiment. It could be part of a Peace Centre, as outlined under (a). Moreover, it could be a very hot nucleus for such a Centre.

The students would be expected to learn by participation in research and promotion projects which would be developed as an essential part of the curriculum. The curricular possibilities would include the other projects in this chapter, and numerous others.

(g) *Promoting a National Department of Peace*

For any group with a high degree of courage, we would recommend the launching of a movement for a new department in their national government. In the last chapter we indicated that the ideal organization for peace research would be under international auspices but supported by national governments. Considering the amount of isolationism and international distrust now prevalent, it is possible that a less ideal arrangement might be more feasible. This would be peace research financed by a single nation under its own sponsorship. In 1943, Gardner Murphy suggested:

> The State Department does not, in any serious sense, do research on the prevention of war. Nevertheless, it is to be hoped that some of the war-time activities of the State Department, of the various international economic bureaus, and of the Co-ordinator of Inter-American Affairs may possibly establish in Washington—or in the public mind—the notion that serious, large-scale research on international affairs is the government's obligation.
>
> *Human Nature and Enduring Peace*

And in 1949 Alexander Leighton said:

> There might be a unit in the federal government that carried out the continuous collection and analysis of information on the causal factors underlying international animosities and international cooperation.
>
> *Human Relations in a Changing World*

David Hinshaw has discussed this ideal at great length in his book *Sweden: Champion of Peace*. He writes:

> Even so, there does not exist in the entire world one single government that contains an officially created, sponsored and financially supported peace department. 'Total' war and 'total' peace both require understanding of 'total' society....
>
> The principal duties of our state department are confined to the formulation, interpretation and application of our foreign policy. From the point of view of peace, its hands are tied in a measure by having to co-ordinate its policies and activities with those of the Department of National Defense, whose policies are made and directed by men whose business it is to make war bigger and better. The point stands out like a sore thumb that neither the State Department nor any of the others is equipped or qualified to direct the study or to apply the findings or to perform the duties of a department of peace....
>
> A department of peace and education might, at comparatively small cost, open up new roads to peace:
> 1. by co-ordinating the information now in hand;
> 2. by gaining additional information that would help to strengthen and advance the peace movement;
> 3. to serve as a symbol to all men everywhere of our serious, determined purpose to realize the peace ideal.
>
> The dollar cost of an official peace department in our government, as compared with war's cost will be infinitesimal.... Today supporting the war way with physical science, man stands on the brink of self-annihilation, where 'dreadful war shall answer his demand.' Today, if he will support the peace way with the social sciences, he may yet realize his glory and fulfill his promise.

National sponsorship of international research might have the disadvantage of actual or suspected partisan bias. Some of this could be offset if the organization were to be staffed by persons from almost all nations. Surely the logic for such a department is high even though the precedent for it be low. It is assumed by the author that such a department would operate primarily as an organism for enlightenment and understanding through research. Its first and most basic job would be to find out how to achieve peace. A resolution favouring a National Department of Peace, headed by a Secretary with cabinet rank, was introduced in the 83rd Congress of the United States.

The first step in a project for promoting such a movement

might well be extensive survey of opinion or potential sentiment among various types of persons—laymen, political experts, practising politicians, etc. Such a survey might reveal the probability of success of such a project, the type of resistance to such a movement, and some of the most needed early steps.

Summary

In this chapter we have not attempted to furnish the reader with a large variety of isolated tasks from which he could choose his random activities. Rather, we have attempted to indicate the nature of a possible grass-roots process. Like all other profound and democratic proposals, the point of view developed here may be low in the number of people to whom it will at first appeal. We have presented it because we think it rates very high in the scale of effectiveness if and when acted upon. The most hazardous aspect of our proposals for action is that which calls upon the individual to initiate—to lead off and not wait for others to act first. How many people there are who are socially adequate for this role we cannot tell. These potential pioneers may be common men with an uncommon degree of 'common' sense. They must have enough courage to break appreciably with their past. Old habits of feeling, of thinking, of acting, will not suffice.

No one should inhibit his action because his resources of time or money or social influence may be much more limited than those of someone else. The essential operation is for each person to appraise his own resources and the degree of his practical interest and validly match both with realistic appropriation.

12
RÉSUMÉ

THE essential thesis presented in this book can be expressed in the twofold statement that mankind does not now possess the knowledge necessary for a speedy and deliberate elimination of the unbearable curse of war, but that a redirection of our intellectual resources might quickly produce this knowledge. Let us make a less brief summary under the following 17 propositions.

1. *Humanity is at a crisis.* It will either go ahead or go under. Our danger is unprecedented. It accelerates. The sudden disappearance of the species has recently become a possibility. Hundreds of millions of us are unitedly and co-operatively arrayed against hundreds of millions of others of us. Our capacity for destruction increases hourly. No remedy is in sight. But there is no point in giving up. There is still a *chance* for the human race to reach a destiny endlessly progressive and far grander than anything we have yet known. But the crisis must be met.

2. *The crisis is cultural.* Cultural collapse is not certain. Neither is cultural recovery and progress. The question now is shall we suddenly return to the jungle or will cultural evolution continue upward and forward to new and unimaginable levels? Will confidence and compassion and co-operation win out over fear and cruelty and conflict? Will improved law and order hold the line against mounting violence and eventual chaos? Will present organization for large-scale antagonism between mammoth political segments of society be supplanted by an over-all wholeistic human unity?

Parts of our plight are modern. Parts of it have been long in the making—imbedded deep in our history. It is in our poetry and in our art, in our philosophy and our religion. The total pattern of human values is full of confusions and contradictions. We strain our emotions to extend our sympathies and exert our intelligence to relieve suffering, combat disease, and delay death. But we deliberately (in the name of security) cultivate hysterias of hostility. We use the utmost of our intelligence to uncover the secrets of total destruction. Our culture is not totally bad, but badly mixed. Many, if not most of its elements, are not bad in themselves, but the total net effect is that of a very dynamic culture moving with ever greater speed in dangerous directions.

Our progress is increasingly out of balance. The science of physical relations is daily giving to an unbalanced culture more and more of that of which it already has relatively too much, namely, physical power. Daily a long overdue science of human relations for giving us greater social harmony is being neglected. Discovery of the secret of atomic energy has unfortunately preceded the discovery of world unity through world government or otherwise.

Cultural evolution, however, need not be left to chance. And we do not have to wait for biological evolution to change human nature. Its change was not required to get us in the fix we are in. But man will have to take greater responsibility for man's destiny if the culture is to go up and on instead of down and under.

3. *The crisis is that of a sick society.* Our affliction is more social than personal. The crux of our new and alarming situation can better be accounted for in our social complexities than in our personal perversities. Our great society, made possible by great science and technology, has become enormously organized, but imperfectly so, and to a critical degree. Our institutions are dynamic and efficient, but their total pattern is tragically incomplete and inadequate. Our most conscientious services are rendered to massive institutions operating in a pattern of conflict and mutual frustration.

Social organization, however, is a human function and should be susceptible of improvement. If we are misorganized we can reorganize, granted that we discover with objective clarity and appropriate unanimity the secret of what changes are possible and needed and how they can be brought about. These changes will have to be accompanied by changes in our attitudes, particularly our attitudes towards our institutions.

4. *The immediate critical issue is the institution of war*—its continuation versus its elimination. Will man eliminate war before war eliminates man? The issue is not this or that particular war, but war *in toto*—not war postponement but war eradication. Peace is not merely the absence of war but a dynamic process

whose characteristics include the *absence of war preparation*. Unless war preparations cease in every nation there is no peace. The focus of the crisis is on the outcome of the race between the unifying and the disunifying processes in our total culture— between our ability to organize for international harmony and global co-operation and our propensity to organize for hostility and antagonism. Our culture has and will have other problems, but our crucial problem now is the problem of international conflict associated with national loyalty. Our sociology has and will have other and profound problems, but the problem now is war versus non-violent techniques of settling conflicts at the international level. It is folly to talk of cultural evolution and to hope for positive social reorganization unless we can quickly evolve to forestall the misorganization for violence which threatens to end both our culture and our society and possibly our race. War eradication is our first great universal must. But the issue still hangs in the balance Neither war nor peace is inevitable.

5. *War is a human activity*. It is perpetuated by human decision, permitted by human acquiescence and neglect, and made deadly by human invention. Guns are invented by human heads and made by human hands. The triggers are pulled by human fingers. The air is full of scape-goats and alibis. The pot calls the kettle black, but the fact remains that war, though inhumane, is distinctly human. It has been well said, 'Men do not want war, but want what causes war'. Surely in the long run we do not want what war causes.

6. *Men potentially have a deep desire for peace*. The potential passion for peace can be as deep as the desire for survival which is potentially as real as the total passion for life. It is buttressed by the urge of evolution itself. The makings of this passion for peace are as real as individual sanity and interpersonal compassion. 'Love is as real as hate.' Of goodwill there is more than is usually apparent—more than has ever been released. Why the non-release? Why does modern man tolerate the slaughterous and fatal institution of modern war? Why does he not get rid of it?

7. *Man's potential passion for peace is forestalled by the lack of adequate knowledge*. The individual man is caught in the trap of a social process which he did not originate but in which he is a functioning factor. He is a part of a great society afflicted with a dynamic cancer whose cure is as yet undiscovered. We have

fallen into a process of seeking security through threat and counter-threat. The interactive process of social or political psychology seems beyond our understanding, and hence beyond our control. Few men seem to be clearly aware of this ignorance. It seems to be obscured by our proneness to indulge in mutual incrimination. Too often the assumption operates that no remedy is possible because of human perversity rather than the more hopeful assumption that we have merely not discovered the remedy. We propose that here as elsewhere the possession of an adequate pattern of hopeful action could turn peace wish into peace will and resolution. This is a universal principle and constitutes no slander upon human motivation.

8. *Absence of a solution demands search for the solution.* As intellectual honesty requires the admission of ignorance of the remedy, so moral courage requires the search for the remedy. The biggest item in the time schedule of progress in solving a real problem is the time required to recognize the problem and to make up one's mind to attack it in real earnest. This is the most hopeful answer to the query of how to make the best use of whatever time remains—namely, search for the method of how to get rid of war. There are many other problems for human intelligence to tackle but they can wait.

But what are the characteristics of a hopeful search—what conditions are likely to bring success?

9. *The search must be scientific.* It must be carried on with the utmost use of human intelligence. The situation calls for search and research unrelenting and systematic. We dare leave no stone unturned. All aspects of human behaviour must be scrutinized—political, religious, economic, artistic, emotional, intellectual—all human processes and institutions must come under survey. The research must be done with open minds. Rigid adherence to inflexible absolutes and fixed faith in untested intuitions will frustrate the search. The findings must be transferable from searcher to searcher and eventually to the whole of the human family. The sudden creative insights from the mystic's mountain are useless unless and until translatable to the many. The discoveries must be suited to wide acceptability—sufficiently wide to make genuine co-operation possible. To this end the search must be carried on in the spirit, not of those who are trying to win a propaganda campaign, but of those who are trying to find the democratic solution

to a common problem of universal concern. This means that the search must be objective in spirit and method. The causes of war as well as the causes of peace may be highly subjective, but their *detection* requires the exercise of great rationality. The cure, when it comes, may contain a crucial measure of emotion, but the search must contain a large measure of the judicious and the circumspect. The controlling and common motive must be that of universal advantage through social harmony—all-inclusive human unity.

But scientific search has to be provided for.

10. *The search requires a new division of labour.* Each public service is rendered by some of us—not all of us. 'What is everybody's business is nobody's business.' It is impossible for everyone to make the search. But it could be done easily (or at least feasibly) by *proxy*. Successful pursuit of a goal so elusive as world peace requires the full time—the undivided attention—of wholehearted and unhampered and expert searchers. That there is today no appreciable number of such workers is not the fault of any one of us but of all of us. It is a tragic oversight of our total society. We can expect discoveries only if we arrange for appropriate discoverers.

11. *The search must be sizeable and soon.* The division of labour must be large enough to meet the demands of the problem. When a moderately cynical realist is asked about his hopes for peace, a common answer is 'Maybe, in a thousand years'. This could be true if there were that much time left; and if cultural evolution moved as slowly in the next as in the last 1,000 years; and if it had to continue undirected by human intelligence and unaided by human resolution. On the contrary it is later than many think. The discovery of peace must come soon or not at all. We cannot afford to wait for the sciences of human relations to evolve as slowly as did the sciences of physical relations, especially not the science of peace.

Scientific speed is directly correlated with scientific manpower. Our immediate destiny is compounded of three variables: time, distance, and speed. The time is short, the distance is great. We have only one option in this formula and that is in the number of men we choose to put on the job. The situation demands not only full-time workers fully trained, but hundreds of thousands of them. In the cold war effort in certain countries the number of war personnel is as high as one worker out of every five. A sizeable percentage of this number is scientific personnel, perpetually searching out the secrets of greater destruction. A half million scientific workers searching to make war obsolete would be less than one person out of a thousand of the world's working population.

But how can these workers be mandated?

12. *The searchers must be salaried.* Practically no division of labour in the world's economy is without wages. If we are ever to have an adequate division of labour for peace, the worker must be conceived of as 'worthy of his hire'. A task so difficult and so indispensable cannot be entrusted to people who have to spend most of their time and energy at other activities in order to earn a living. The economic blockade to individual peace action, scientific or otherwise, must not be evaded. We must carefully spell out the implications of its recognition.

13. *Peace must be paid for.* Money has to be earmarked. Billions of dollars may be needed for the sustaining fees for hundreds of thousands of continuous workers. War preparation costs hundreds of billions, and war itself trillions. Why should we expect peace at the price of a few paltry millions or less? War is big business. This is because, in millions of instances, war pays. If peace is ever to be the major business of any considerable number of people, it too must have its pay aspects. The price cannot long and further be postponed. Realistic peace budgets have to be created. Deliberate peace must be deliberately paid for. The work can be and probably will have to be done by a few, but the dollars can be paid by the many. The cost *per capita*, if widely shared by the world's population, may be exceedingly small, but we must be very careful that our desire to exact a just share from everyone does not result in our failure to get it from anyone. Let us not lose our birthright to survival through quibbling over who pays for the pottage.

14. *The first search is search for research funds.* No other bottleneck to peace research is at once so clear and realistic as is the financial. Note the blueprint dilemma. On every hand we are met with the demand for a blueprint—a plan as to how the research will be conducted—before theoretical and practical support is forthcoming. At the same time, the planning of the research on a problem so long neglected, on a scale sufficient to meet the

urgencies of the hour, is one that requires a tremendous amount of thought and time of a large number of individuals who can approach it without haste and without distraction. Such men do not now exist, and will not exist until provision is made to take care of their grocery bills. But this in turn requires at least an initial and small, and not too small, budget. In other words the plan demanded for the money power requires itself manpower which is not available without the money. The solution of the problem of financing the researchers must come early and not late in the total schedule.

15. *A new pattern of faith is required.* Anything new or additional in human behaviour requires something new or additional in human faith. Increased faith both in science and in democracy is essential. Democracy must be conceived as a realizable and dynamic ideal rather than as a past achievement. Science must be conceived as capable, not only of new distances, but also of new directions. Realization of a science of human relations including a science of peace, requires greater faith in (*a*) the potentials of harmony and co-operation among individuals and nations; (*b*) the endless power of a never-ending revelation of new and ever more relevant facts; (*c*) the elastic resource of human intelligence whose possibilities we have scarcely begun to realize; (*d*) the creative possibilities to adapt old and create new methods for solving unsolved problems, both old and new; and, (*e*) the capacity of human emotion to give humane direction to human reason. All this means increased faith in man—in man's intellectual reliability and in his social reliability. Separate faiths in science and in democracy are not enough. Their combination is essential. The crisis in our culture calls for faith in the merging of curiosity with compassion—of love of truth with love of man.

Now the social process we have been envisioning requires idealistic and realistic pioneers with special courage. As requisite to the courage to remove the mountains of financial barriers to a scientific peace movement there is need to emphasize one special psychological factor, which follows.

16. *A special confidence in social support is required.* This, too, is a faith—a sort of faith in faith—a faith in the good faith of others. The only persons who can touch off a chain reaction for a scientific search for peace are those who not only believe but

believe there are others who believe—enough others to make a movement possible. It is not enough to care about peace. We must assume that there are others who care. If none are willing to make this assumption, all is lost. The 'war' against war cannot be won without strong morale. Our Achilles' heel is here. Our ability to pull together to remove the financial bottleneck to a scientific movement for peace is widely blocked by the assumption in the individual that he is the only individual who believes in such a movement and cares enough for peace to pay a realistic portion of the price. Good will is inhibited by fear of its absence. 'People don't want peace.' 'Others will not co-operate with you.' These propositions are met in almost any circle where serious peace research is proposed. Here lies dangerous truth. It is true that a great many will not co-operate—at least not at the outset. But we must find those who will.

The more courageous and confident must intercommunicate. The pioneers need to become mutually aware of each other's existence and identity. The strain on one's credulity becomes gradually lessened with each new evidence that others are ready and willing. Of all misunderstandings or non-understandings, the first to be removed are those among the promoters or prospective promoters of this movement.

17. *The individual must decide—decide to act—to act co-operatively.* Each socially confident individual must come to decision for personal action. If anything is accomplished it will only be accomplished through the personal decision and commitment of individuals. He who has the courage and the concern must make up his own mind to invest and to advertise both modestly and courageously his investment and his concern and his willingness to confer. Great co-operation is required. But co-operation requires and includes individual decision and action. .

Peace is indivisible. It is international peace that is discussed in this manuscript, i.e., world peace. When it comes it must come to all. It must exist universally or not at all. This is not true of its causation—at least not the scientific beginnings of its causation. Honest decision to contribute can be made anywhere, anytime, by anyone with concern and social imagination. Democratic disarmament will require wide unanimity. Not so with disarmament research.

The challenge of the universal ignorance which tyrannizes over us all can make its first appeal to a sensitive and alert few. These few can save the many if they be confident, and if they intercommunicate.

POSTSCRIPT
to Second Printing

The total diplomatic world picture has not brightened since the first printing of this book. This is not surprising when we consider the astounding imbalance between the total human intellectual investment in the cause of war and the cause of peace. In the pursuit of security through armaments the nations are expending upwards of one hundred billion dollars per year. Toward peace the nations are spending niggardly or not at all. In the past few years, however, there have occurred small but hopeful beginnings.

In 1959 there was officially established at the University of Michigan the Center for Research on Conflict Resolution, through which scholars and dollars can be brought together both in residence and in absentia for purposes of research of real relevance to peace. The *Journal of Conflict Resolution,* a quarterly for research related to war and peace, promoted by the same nucleus of scholars and now a part of the Center, is now in its fifth year. It is the first interdisciplinary journal of its kind. Also in 1959 the Institute for International Order launched a relatively ambitious program of research exploration in five areas—Arms Control, Economics of Disarmament, Political Decision Making, World Rule of Law, and Communication and Attitude. Reports on these, comprising several hundred pages and presenting nearly five hundred research proposals, are obtainable from the Institute at 11 West 42nd Street, New York 36. The Institute also launched, under the editorship of Dr. Larry Leonard, a quarterly digest, *Current Thought on Peace and War,* now edited and published from the International Rule of Law

POSTSCRIPT TO SECOND PRINTING 195

Center at Duke University. Reference to the issues of this digest will give the reader knowledge of current publications and programs and organizations related to peace. Early in 1961 there was established a new Peace Research Institute at Washington, D. C., with the Honorable James Wadsworth as Director. Other significant developments include programs in International Relations at Northwestern University, Washington University in St. Louis, as well as Harvard, Duke, Massachusetts Institute of Technology, Columbia, and other universities in the United States; a new Department for Conflict and Peace Research as a division of the Institute for Social Research in Oslo, Norway; and a development toward more intense research by the Grotius Seminar at The Hague, Netherlands.

Under the Kennedy Administration in Washington there is considerable promise of a new department of disarmament for the purpose of planning and research. Some of us are *hoping* that such a department can grow rapidly and successfully avoid partisan distortions due to the Cold War. Similar developments in other national governments have not come to the notice of this writer.

Two specifically recommended brief publications dealing with research planning and research promoting are *The Bridge of Reason* by Norman Z. Alcock of Oakville, Ontario, Canada, and "Long Range Program for Research in International Relations" by Harold Guetzkow of Northwestern University. The former contains a plan for a network of peace research institutes in a number of nations.

Some of the aforementioned beginnings are directly attributable to participation and leadership inspired by the reading of this volume—inspiration resulting in one instance of a very definitely earmarked contribution of $100,000 and in another instance of 60,000 guilders. These scattered and all-too-infrequent occurrences support the assumption that there exists a potential will to supply the essentials of the science of peace.

Over the past seven years there has been no abatement of the urgency of the need for a mammoth, objective, non-partisan scientific attack upon the problem of war. Correspondence as well as face-to-face dialogue has continuously served to emphasize the importance of a better process for the discovery and intercommunicating of those persons who are willing to invest adequate amounts of their time and intelligence and material substance towards the realization of this scientific goal. For the further discovery of these "critical few" the author solicits the reader's cooperation. In every instance where additional readers and proponents have been brought to light and together there has been an intermediary agent, either personal or institutional. These potential participants are of many types—scientist and non-scientist, scholarly and non-scholarly, wealthy and not wealthy, those of major and those of minor influence—any who believe that men can have a part in man's survival.

Together we may yet avert the tide of madness which threatens to engulf our civilization. Let us act upon our faith in man and his destiny. For purposes of moral support we need to become more fully aware of each other. You are invited to send your reactions, your questions, or your positive and constructive suggestions to

> THEO. F. LENTZ, *Director*
> Peace Research Laboratory
> 5937 Enright Avenue
> St. Louis 12, Missouri
> USA